I USED TO HAVE WINGS

DAMION PLATT

ISBN - 978-0992066710
I AM NOT A STATUE PUBLICATIONS
For Information, questions, comments or help writing and
illustrating your own book: Email **Damion.Platt@gmail.com** or
Omarrwill@gmail.com

Dedicated to my mother who has always been my sunrise even when she was stormy.

Special thanks to all the special people in my life. I love you guys so very much and could not have written this novel without you.

Delroy, Angella, Kathleen (grandma), Kadeen, Shantel, Kaciann, Elaine, Robert, Paula, Fiona, Omarr, Ciann, Melisa, Kimberly, Alicia, Alisha, Tyrone, Jemal, Krystle, Claire, Siobhan, Wayne, Ryan, Angie, Shey, Sonya, Lucien, Dave, Rodel, Karla,

CHAPTER 1

TIME
(Vanessa)

On earth, you have been granted a finite amount of time and
energy in which to smile, laugh, love, live, learn, and
accomplish your purpose. It is imperative that you appreciate
every moment of your life; never allow the sorrows of a second
to rob you of the joys of an hour.
-
Teach us to number our days that we may get a heart of
wisdom.

Psalm 90:12

****

His coarse bass filled voice chips away at me, each grisly
syllable cutting into me like a sharp axe abusing the base of an
already feeble tree.
*'You're fat, you're ugly. You're fat and ugly and nobody will
ever love you.'*
His words, although more than ten years old, still sting and
cut deep as though they are harassing my ears for the first
time.
"He's right," I sigh, placing my right hand on my protruding
stomach and shamefully squeezing pounds of soft flesh as I
stare at a reflection of myself in a tall, wide, grocery store
mirror. "I am fat... I am ugly. I am the fattest, ugliest, woman in
the world."
Shaking my head contentiously, I struggle and fight until
my mind breaks free from his calloused grip Once free, I
remind myself that unlike other overweight women who are
overweight because they have no self-control, I am overweight
because it was the one and only way for me to gain control.

I bite my bottom lip in anger and then shake my head again in hopes of regaining complete control of my chaotic mind.

I'm not overweight.

Overweight isn't real.

Overweight is a fictitious concept created by a hateful, abusive, ignorant society.

How can I be overweight?

How can anyone be overweight or underweight?

Whose weight would they be over, whose weight would they be under?

I grunt and grumble under my breath.

He and my mother ruined my life. They took control of my brain when I was too young to resist their influence and now even as an adult I can't rid myself of them. No matter what I do, no matter how many times I kick them out of my mind they always return, coming back louder and stronger than before.

I clench my fists.

I hate my mother.

I hate my uncle.

I wish I could kil-

Suddenly, a man's loud and obnoxious laugh fills my ears, pulling me from my thoughts of murder and revenge.

"I swear, suicide has never looked so sweet and delicious. It almost makes me want to break my diet."

When I turn around there is a tall, chocolate skinned man with long dreadlocks standing in front of me. He is wearing a grey fitted three-piece suit, a crisp white dress shirt, a solid black tie and freshly polished black shoes. On his right index finger is a bright yellow gold ring encrusted with what appears to be small diamonds. He looks like one of those people who love life, one of those happy silver spooned rich people who have never felt pain and who have ruined other people's lives in order to obtain fortune and fame.

There are no stress lines or wrinkles on his face.

His teeth are white and pristine.

His hair is glowing, his posture is perfect and he smells... he smells the way that all happy people smell.

I despise people like him, people who prosper by doing horrible things and yet they seem to receive no punishment for their misdeeds. They drive around in their fancy cars and they wear their fancy clothes, and they live in their big fancy houses and go on their expensive fancy vacations meanwhile good and honest people like me are forced to live from paycheque to paycheque. Good people like me suffer so that evil people like him can be happy.

I hope something horrible happens to him. I hope he gets a disease that makes all his blood money useless, I hope his boat crashes or his mansion burns down. I hope he gets what he deserves.

"Forgive me," he smiles, once again revealing his perfect row of chalk white dentally enhanced teeth. "I didn't mean to disturb you. I was just thinking aloud... too loud I guess," he laughs.

I roll my eyes, turn my back to him and place a multi-coloured bag of Jellybeans and a blue box of Twinkies into my shopping cart.

I love Twinkies, I started eating them when-

"My name is Shariffe Shakur," he says. "And if you have a minute to spare, I'd like to introduce myself to you."

I try to ignore him and continue shopping but I can feel him behind me, eyeing me down. His presence makes me uneasy, it is heavy and overwhelming, it feels as if someone is holding a large boulder over my head and is threatening to drop it on me the moment I do or say the wrong thing.

"Hello..." he clears his throat, brutish and loud. "Excuse me... Hi."

I continue to ignore him.

"Excuse me... Ma'am... Can you hear me?"

I take a deep breath and attempt to steady my mind and my heart meanwhile continuing to pretend as if the bizarre man behind me does not exist.

"I'll pay for it," he says in the most patriarchal and derogatory tone I have ever heard. "How much does it cost? What's your price? Name it and I'll pay it."

I whip around and face the stranger in the grey suit; my eyes and lips contorted in disgust and shock.

"Excuse me!" I exclaim. "What did you just say to me?"

He raises his eyebrows, lets out an egotistical laugh and stares at me as if I'm the one who is crazy, "I want to buy some of your time. How much will I have to pay? What's your price?"

I can't believe what is happening right now but this is the world I live in, a world where men think women are objects that they can purchase and use as they see fit.

"I'm not for sale," I grimace.

"That's good to know," he grins. "But I don't want to buy you, I want to buy some of your time."

I shake my head and roll my eyes, candidly displaying my annoyance, "no part of me is for sale."

I grip the red plastic handle of my shopping cart and storm past the stranger.

Men are disgusting, they literally live to objectify and belittle everything they come in contact with.

"One minute is all I need," he says, pulling up along side me and matching my strides perfectly. "And when my minute is up I'll leave you alone, I swear it."

"No," I say, my voice swift and sharp.

"Think about it," he responds. "The time it is taking you to ignore and deny my request is actually greater than the time it will take you to accept my request. If two minutes ago you had just sold me a minute of your time I would have been finished by now and you would be free of me," he smiles.

I stop walking.

I turn and look him in his face.

"One minute and then you'll leave me alone, you promise?"

He nods his head yes.

"Fine," I say, my tone heavy with disdain. "One minute but that's it."

"How much?"

"I don't want your money," I half scream. "Listen," I compose myself. "You don't have to pay me, just say what you need to say and then leave me alone."

He shakes his head, "no, I'm sorry, I do have to pay you. Please," he says softly, his eyes fixed on my eyes. "What's your price?"

His eyes are soft but stern and I can see in them an immutable world of crazy, a world that refuses to be invaded by outside forces, he will not relent unless I agree to his conditions.

I let out a breath of air and then awkwardly say, "Fi.. Forty... Fifty? Fifty-dollars..."

Without hesitation he reaches into his back pocket, pulls out a grey money clip and hands me a blood red fifty-dollar bill. I shake my head and place the money in my pocket. I can't believe I just lowered myself to the level of a common street prostitute who sells her time for money. Suddenly, my mother's voice rises in my head and she tells me that I should have charged the man more for my time. She tells me that I am an idiot, that I am undervaluing myself and that I should always bargain with men because men will always pay the minimum unless you force them to pay the maximum. I push my mother out from my head and focus on the crazy man.

"How can I help you in sixty seconds?"

"Come home with me," he says flatly. "I need-"

"Here!" The word flies from my mouth, nearly taking my tongue with it. "Take back your money and leave me alone."

He shakes his head in a calm and collected manner. "You don't have to answer right now, take some time and think about my request and then contact me."

From his wallet he withdraws a matte white business card and attempts to hand it to me.

"I don't need to think about anything, my answer is no and my answer will always be no," I say, refusing his little white card. "So please just take back your money and leave me alone. I don't want any strings attached."

"Please," he says solemnly. "Do as you wish you wish with the card once I have left but for now just humor me. And regarding the money it belongs to you. I gave you fifty-dollars and you're giving me a minute of your time that was our agreement and there are no strings beyond that, I give you my word. If you don't want to keep the money, donate it."

I sigh and place the card in my pocket along with the cash. I'll throw it away later... the card not the cash.

Without warning the stranger pulls up the sleeves of his grey blazer and begins to transfer the contents of his shopping cart into my shopping cart, crushing my bags of candy and my boxes of pastries with his fruits, vegetables, and packs of fresh cut Salmon.

"What is wrong with you?! What are you doing? Are you crazy?"

He pauses, his hands cradling a large bundle of carrots, and a bag of dark green avocadoes, "Your food should be your medicine and your medicine should be your food."

I shake my head, grunt, and glance down at my watch.

The stranger has fifteen seconds left.

When he is gone I will throw away his business card and reshelf everything or leave the unwanted food at the register before cashing out.

Sixteen seconds later, once he has completed his peculiar task of offloading the contents of his shopping cart to my cart the strange man turns and walks away from me without so much as a goodbye. As I stare into the depths of my now fruit and vegetable filled shopping cart my right eye begins to twitch sporadically, alerting me that something is wrong or something is about to go horribly wrong.

I take a deep breath, steady my nerves, and speed walk to the register, glancing from side to side as I go. When I arrive at the checkout counter there is tall, skinny, caramel skinned girl with long hair, soft hazel eyes, and long curly eyelashes standing behind the register.

She is beautiful.

I would have looked like her at her age if I didn't have to overeat to survive.

She smiles at me.

I smile at her.

Placing all of my groceries onto the conveyor belt I wait for her to scan my items before handing her the fifty-dollar bill that the strange man gave to me. She looks at the money and then looks back at me. She tries to hide what she is doing but I can see it in her eyes... she is judging me.

"Ma'am, it's ok... your... umm...your friend has already paid for everything," she hands me back the red fifty dollar bill. "What would you like to do with your change ma'am?"

"What?"

The girl rolls her eyes before releasing a frustrated breath of air, "Your friend paid for everything already and he said that if there was any change left over I should ask you what to do with it."

"Friend? What are you talking about, what friend?"

"Your tall friend with the dreads."

I grimace.

"What would you like to do with your change, ma'am?"

"Do whatever you want with it, it's not my money."

"Anything I want?" she says, her eyes growing wide.

"Yes."

"Are you sure ma'am? It's... a lot... of change," she whispers.

"Yes, I'm sure."

She stares at me long and hard before quickly glancing around the store and stuffing a handful of green and blue cash into her right pant's pocket.

"Sooo, is he single?"

I stop packing my groceries and look her stern in the eyes.

"Is who single?"

"Your friend," she smiles

"He's not my friend," I declare sharply.

She raises her eyebrows in shock, "Wow... you mean he's your," she gasps. "Wow Ma'am... you are really lucky. I wish I had a man like him. All the boys my age are broke idiots, they always want me to pay for everything. Nobody I've dated has ever bought me groceries. I bet you never have to pay for anything. He must be really rich; he had on a Paul Newman yellow gold Rolex, a 24k gold ring with diamonds and an Alexander Price suit. I didn't get to see his shoes but I'm sure they were expensive. Ohhh, I wish-"

"How old are you?" I cut in, silencing her mindless rant.

"19... Why?" Her eyes go wide with expectation. "Does he have a friend or a younger brother? Can you hook me up??"

I shake my head, pack my bags and exit the grocery store without saying another word or glancing at the foolish child.

CHAPTER 2

REST

(Vanessa)

We all have felt the burdens of a life that seems to be falling
apart; we all have felt the unyielding need for rest and for
peace.

-

"I will satisfy the weary soul, and every languishing soul I will
replenish."

Jeremiah 31:25
****

I open my front door and enter my small cramped apartment. It
should be a crime to make building units this small; I am
basically living in a walk-in-closet with a washroom and a
kitchenette. As I make my way to the section of my home that is
supposed to pass for a kitchen I hear them hissing and
scattering across the floor, trying their best to escape my non-
existent wrath. They hide in the crevices and the dark parts of
my apartment where beams of light and the thin bristles of my
broomstick cannot reach. They first arrived five years ago,
sneaking around in the shadows and breeding in private until
the thin walls and cheap hardwood flooring could no longer
contain them. Eventually, they spilled out onto my kitchen tile,
climbed up out of my sinks and descended out from the vents
that were supposed to be funnelling clean air into my home.
They have lived with me for over five years and yet still they
run and hide from me. You would think by now that they would
realize that I don't care enough about them to want to kill them.
If I wanted them dead they would all be dead. I know exactly
where they gather and lay their eggs. If I wanted to be cruel I
could flood their hideouts and their nests with rubbing alcohol

mixed with sea salt and kill them instantly but they don't bother me so I don't bother them... live and let live. Besides, I'm going to move out of this horrid apartment soon... I won't be here forever.

After packing away my groceries, I head straight to my bedroom. With the lights turned off, slow music playing, the curtains drawn and the door closed, my tiny room feels like a distant world that has yet to be infiltrated by other people's wants and desires. In my room I am completely alone. The only person who bothers me while I'm in here is myself. I still haven't discovered how to turn off my thoughts. I've tried meditation, medication, soft music, loud music and more medication but nothing has worked so far.

Last week I purchased a new mattress, one of those fancy tempur-pedic foam mattresses that conform to your body. It makes me feel as if I'm sleeping on a perfectly shaped cloud. And although my new mattress does not have the power to deactivate my overactive thoughts it does relax my body enough for me to fall asleep quicker than normal, and sometimes sleep is all I have. For the sake of my sanity, I am often forced to close my eyes and escape reality.

As I unbutton my pants I feel the strange man's business card pricking my thigh as if it were fighting to gain my attention. I reach into my pocket and withdraw the small piece of sharp paper and read it.

"... Sha...Shhariffe Shak...ur." His name rolls awkwardly off my lips. "...Lawyer?" I laugh aloud at the obviously fake business card.

Did he really think typing lawyer on a small piece of paper would fool me into believing that he was safe to go home with? Being a lawyer just means he is more dangerous; he can kill me and then defend himself in court.

I toss the business card to one side of my room and watch it as it falls to the ground. Something tells me to pick it up, rip it into tiny indistinguishable pieces and then throw it in the garbage but I don't listen to that thing.

Hopefully the cockroaches will eat it while I'm sleeping.

I finish undressing, take a warm shower, and then curl up on my bed in the foetal position. While waiting for the softness of my mattress to calm my body I think about the strange man from the grocery store along with a documentary that I watched a couple of months back. The documentary was about Canada's most notorious serial killers and the women who fell in love with them. According to this documentary 1 out of every 10,000 women across Canada has at one point or another been hopelessly beguiled by a serial killer.

The most dangerous of all the Canadian killers was a man named Leonard Diopold, also known as the Mississauga Monster. Diopold was a tall, beautiful, man with light green eyes, olive tanned skin and long golden blond hair that stopped precisely at his right and left earlobes. His cheekbones were like divinely chiselled mountains and his lips were thin and yet full of expression and life. He dressed like a male model, only wearing tailored suits and deep V-neck t-shirts, he was soft spoken, eloquent and moved with a grace and poise that perfectly masked the devil that lived within him. His first reported murder took place on the 17th of May 1989. The victim was a recently divorced and heartbroken 48-year-old Gwen Lucken. Diopold stalked Gwen for months, gathering information on her before approaching and luring the melancholic middle-aged white woman into his clutches by pretending to be a professional photographer who was deeply intrigued by her 'unique' brand of beauty. He took snapshots of Gwen in the grocery store with an old camera that contained no film. After a few minutes of fake pictures and hordes of compliments Diopold informed Gwen that he wanted to take more pictures of her but he needed to do so in an organic environment, an environment that mimicked her natural beauty perfectly. Flattered, lonely, and in need of attention Gwen grabbed hold of the opportunity. Together She and Diopold drove to a derelict farm where for hours Diopold mocked, ridiculed and abused Gwen before taking her life.

Four years and thirteen victims later Diopold was finally apprehended. While being arrested he reportedly told police officers that he should not be arrested or face any kind of punishment because he had not done anything wrong. According to Diopold he was doing the ladies he killed a favour, according to Diopold these women hated their lives and wanted to be free... so he set them free.

CHAPTER 3

THOUGHTS
(Andrew)

The mind does nothing more and nothing less than what you allow.

-

Do not be conformed to this world, but be transformed by the renewal of your mind, that by testing you may 'discern' what is the will of God, what is good and acceptable and perfect.

Romans: 12:2
****

Old age is the devil. Old age is the cruellest curse that an infinitely wise God could devise. Old age sours life, old age turns all that was once sweet medicine into bitter putrid poison. When you become old the world changes, the world that once embraced you and told you to touch, taste, feel and enjoy now tells you to sit in a corner and wait for death.

I take a deep breath and force my mind to think of better times. On the brown coffee table in front of me there sits a small pink bible with the word Angel etched deeply into the skin of its front cover. I can still remember the glow in her eyes and the smile on her face when I first handed that book to her. I wish I could live in that moment forever but I have broken that moment, I have destroyed it beyond repair and-

A loud, sudden, thud at my front door startles me. I turn my aching neck and stare out the square glass window unto my front lawn.

Today, the sun is causing her flawless skin to sparkle like diamonds, her hair is running free and untamed, she is wearing blue shorts and a sleeveless pink top and she is carrying her heavy oversized yellow bag.

I exhale, keeping my eyes on her and following her every move.

Our eyes meet.

I brace myself and attempt to stand to my feet but my weak wrists and my unreliable knees keep me anchored to my seat.

I shake my head in contempt, "I am a happily married man. I love my wife, I love my wife, I love only my wife."

I breathe in and out, waiting for the words to take root in my heart but without my permission my unfaithful thoughts cause my mind to stray from my wife and retreat into the solace of the gorgeous female who is waiting patiently for me just outside of my front door.

'Don't give up,' a strong but soothing voice commands. *'Stand up, stand to your feet, take what you want. Open your door and let her inside, nobody will know… Your wife will never know.'*

CHAPTER 4

NAMES
(Vanessa)

Do not allow the misguided words of others to destroy your
self-love and self-respect.
-
"You shall be called by a new name that the mouth of the Lord
will give. You shall be a crown of beauty in the hand of the
Lord, and a royal diadem in the hand of your God. You shall no
more be termed Forsaken, and your land shall no more be
termed Desolate, but you shall be called My Delight"

Isaiah 62: 2-4
****

It is 9am when my alarm clock sounds, filling my ears with loud
abrasive music. I rollover, tap the snooze button and release a
long tired groan before rising slowly from my bed to prepare for
another horrible day at work.
　My phone rings.
　"Vanessa, please... please, forgive me."
　His voice is hoarse and sounds as if it is clawing and
scratching its way through the tangled phone cord in a
desperate attempt to reach my ears.
　"I'm so sorry Angel," he cries out. "Satan made me do it, I
would never willingly hurt you. I love you, you're my angel but
the devil-"
　I end the call and slam my phone down in a fit of rage and
try to move forward with my day but his voice won't allow me
to move on. His coarse voice abducts me, locks me in a small
dark space and forces me to remember all the horrible things
that I am fighting to forget.
　I hate him!
　I hate people who are like him, people who think that they
can hurt you, people who think they can ruin your life and then

just say sorry. When has sorry ever fixed anything? Sorry doesn't heal lost time, stolen days or bruised skin... sorry is salt on an open wound

'Angel... Angel... Angel,' I repeat the deceitfully clever word in my head before letting out a heated sigh. He used that word like a Trojan horse to gain access to my trust and then the true him came out and destroyed all that I was and all the I had hopes of becoming.

By the time I finish showering and dressing it is 10:15am. 'Satan made me do it, the devil made me do it,' his words flash in my head but before they can overpower me I take a deep breath and push them from my mind and choose to focus on more positive thoughts, like what I'm going to eat for breakfast. Today, I won't have time to stop downtown for a sugar-dog so rummaging through my kitchen cupboards I grab a can of soda, and a strawberry cream-filled Pop-Tart before hurrying out my front door.

The elevator ride to the ground floor is quick.

Outside is beautiful.

The sun is shining.

The sky is blue.

Birds are chirping.

Children are playing.

My car is gone.

My car is gone!!

I scream and let out an exasperated series of long, heavy, tornadoes of air from my mouth before turning around and marching angrily towards the bus stop. My car gets stolen at least once a month by one of these good for nothing kids. They take my car for a joy ride and then they leave it wherever the gas runs out. Every time I find my rust covered car abandoned and devoid of fuel, I can relate.

***

Arriving at work, I stuff the last piece of my strawberry pop-tart into my mouth, chew quickly and then swallow forcefully before pulling open the front door of Ken's Seafood Emporium and rushing inside. My boss, Ken, is standing by the front door waiting for me with an ugly scowl on his face.

"Good morning, Nessy," he says with a fake Scottish accent. "Thank you for deciding to show up," he looks down at his watch. "Four minutes late."

I despise the name Nessy almost as much as I despise the tall skinny Filipino man who is calling me it but for the sake of keeping my job, I don't object or protest his verbal abuse. Nessy is short for Lochness, the gigantic, fat, mythical fish-eating monster that gracelessly swims the serene rivers and lakes of Scotland. When Ken and my co-workers first started referring to me as Nessy I was ecstatic, I thought Nessy was short for Vanessa. I cried for an hour and had to leave work early when I found out what Nessy truly meant but that was over three years ago. Now, I don't let being called Nessy bother me because I know that soon I'll quit this horrible job, I will not be here forever.

I fake smile at Ken and then say, "Good morning, I'm doing great thanks for asking. My car was stolen this morning so I had to take a two-hour bus ride to get here but sorry for being four minutes late. How are you doing today, Ken?"

"Just get to work, Nessy."

"Yes, Ken."

I walk towards him, wanting to grab him by his skinny neck and squeeze it until he can no longer open his mouth to call me Nessy, but I don't do it. Instead, I keep my hands at my sides, walk around him and pass obediently through two large black rubber doors into the dimly lit back of the store. When I am certain that Ken can no longer hear me or see me I grunt, shake my head, roll my eyes and mumble angrily. I raise my hands into the air and I pretend to squeeze his neck until his skin turns red and his eyes close forever, then I let go of him and continue walking down the long black corridor.

At the back of the store there is a large iron door that looks like it belongs in a maximum-security prison, inside of it is a refrigerated room filled with fish.

That is where I work.

I tie my apron around my neck and waist and then pick up my large board handle knife before entering my frozen prison. When I first started working for Ken I looked in the mirror and I promised the young woman looking back at me that this job was beneath her, and therefore was only temporary. Now, after six long years the only joy that I can suck from this horrible job is through pretending that the fish, whose heads I chop off for thirteen dollars an hour, are members of my ex-family.

The big fish are him... the man whose existence was fattened through the slow, daily, agonizing consumption of my existence. The medium sized fish are my mother Jane, and the small insignificant fish are my sister Susan.

The sharp silver blade comes down cutting my mother's head from her body. She doesn't use her head so she doesn't deserve one; men are the head of her life. Next, I grab my sister's skinny, 'perfect,' body and slam it hard onto the cutting board. I want to chop her body into small unrecognizable pieces and then throw her in the garbage but Ken will fire me if I do that.

I hate this job but I need this job.

My blade cuts clean through Susan. I wipe small pieces of her from my face and then exhale two times. A soothing feeling crawls into my veins and begins to fight against the coldness of the room until my entire body feels warm.

I throw Susan's body into a dark green bucket beside my workstation.

I pick up a large, fat, well fed Salt Water Atlantic Salmon and instantly my mind floods with a tempest of horrible memories. Memories that I wish I could cast to the bottom of the ocean.

I place him onto the cutting board, inhale, steady my palpitating heart and then without thought I allow my knife to cut his neck from his body... if only life were this simple.

CHAPTER 5

INDEPENDENCE
(*Vanessa*)

You were not created to live in isolation, to lift the burdens of each day with only two hands or to walk the journey of life with only two feet. You were designed to lift with the power of a community and to journey with the stamina of a family. Unity is key for all of life's successes.

-

"Two are better than one, because they have a good return for their work: If one falls down, his friend can help him up. But pity the man who falls and has no one to help him up!"

Ecclesiastes 4:8-12
****

Sweet smelling clouds of hot white smoke rise quickly from the black iron grill and mix with the humid morning air before slowly disappearing.

I lean forward, inhale happily and then join the long line-up of other hungry customers who are anxiously waiting to sink their teeth into a flame grilled sugar-dog. Sugar-dogs are the newest sensation across Toronto. They are long, thick, cylinders of juicy delicious meat that have been barbecued and then dipped over and over again into a secret sauce and sprinkled with two large handfuls of all-natural brown sugar.

Closing my eyes, I imagine myself biting into a long, juicy, sugar-dog. A soothing sensation shoots up my spine, causing my entire body to shake as the imaginary meat melts in my mouth.

Minutes later, after I have consumed my imaginary meal, I reopen my eyes. What I see overwhelms me and almost causes my heart to stop beating. A tall woman wearing a tight red dress and long black synthetic hair has slipped in front of me in the queue, adding an additional two minutes between my sugar-dog and I. The rage swelling within me is agonizing;

I can feel it ripping through my skin as it charges bullish towards the woman. I want to hurt her, I want to grab her fake hair and throw her out of the line but I control myself.

"Excuse me," I say, my voice high pitched and my face painted with a Barbie-like smile.

The woman doesn't respond to me but I am certain that she has heard me.

I exhale.

"Excuse me," I repeat, politely tapping the woman on her shoulder.

"What?" she half yells, her arms opening wide in indignation as she spins in my direction.

'What?' I think to myself. You just cut in front me and now you have the audacity to ask me what. I should be asking you what. As in what the heck do you think you're doing? What?? I mean isn't it blatantly obvious why I'm tapping you or do you think I just randomly go around tapping people's shoulders for the fun of it?

I take a deep breath, calm myself back down and attempt to speak politely, "Maybe you didn't see me but I was standing in line-"

"And?" she interrupts.

"And..." I scowl while stepping into her personal space. "I'm hungry and I'm also trying to get to work on time. You can't just cut in front of people. Who do you think you are?"

"You snooze you lose."

"You snooze you lose?" I contort my face in disgust. "Are you a child?"

"Yes, you snooze you lose," she repeats her childish idiom but this time sharper and more aggressive. "You were day dreaming, the line started moving forward but you didn't so I cut in front of you that's life, deal with it. You snooze you lose, plus I think you could stand to skip a meal or two," she laughs before turning her back to me.

A nuclear bomb goes off inside of me causing hatred and rage to move through me like a toxic cancer seeking to kill everything around me. Clenching my fists, I narrow my gaze and step aggressively towards the woman. My heart is palpitating and my fingers are shaking with excitement as I reach for the back of the woman's neck.

"I wouldn't do that if I were you," a loud deep-toned voice rings in my ears, causing me to stop inches from tearing the woman to pieces.

I spin around, my hands still tense and ready to attack. The strange, dreadlocked, man from the grocery store is standing there staring at me. He salutes me by placing his right hand on his chest and then gently bowing his head and smiling.

Fear fills me as I back away quickly, creating a safe distance between the stranger and myself.

"Are... are you stalking me?" I say in a panic.

"No, of course not. That is crazy," he laughs.

My heart relaxes slightly, "Th... then," I stutter. "What are you doing here?"

"I'm following you," he smiles.

"What?!" I gasp.

"I'm following you," he repeats the words without fear of judgment, almost as if he believes following women around is a normal everyday activity that he should be free to engage in whenever he chooses.

"You're joking... right?"

"No," he shakes his head. "I'm very serious, actually. Haven't you noticed me? I've been following you everyday since we met at the grocery store."

With the utmost urgency, I allow my mind to wander back to every single place that I've been in the last ten days since meeting him at the grocery store. I don't remember seeing him or anyone who remotely resembles him. Could I have been so disconnected from reality that I wouldn't notice a tall, large, dark skinned man with noticeably long hair following me around?

He must be lying I reassure myself, this must be some sort of sick joke.

"Why are you following me?"

"Down the street from here, there is a nice little restaurant that a friend of mine owns. How about we go and grab a bite to eat and get to know one another? All I need is one hour of your time."

"Are you crazy? Do I look stupid? You just admitted to stalking me and now you expect me to go out to eat with you at some restaurant that your friend owns?"

He studies my face then calmly shakes his head and says in a cool and relaxed tone, "No, you do not look stupid to me and I said I was following you, not stalking you so you have nothing to worry about."

"What's the difference?"

"Well... Stalking is the aggressive and threatening pursuit of an individual and following is the-".

"I didn't actually want to know the difference," I interrupt.

"Then why did you ask?"

I roll my eyes, "It's called a rhetorical-" I stop speaking and grunt. "Why am I explaining anything to you? Listen, just stay away from me. Don't stalk me or follow me or any other thing that involves you being anywhere near me at any time. I don't know you and I don't want to go anywhere with you. Now, please leave me alone."

When I turn back around the skinny, disrespectful, woman whom I was about to tear to pieces is nowhere to be found and there are three new customers now standing in front me. I'm livid but most of all I'm hungry... I'm so very hungry. I can hear my stomach growling and feel my blood boiling as I imagine the rude woman prancing down the street eating what was supposed to be my sugar-dog. I look past the new group of customers and enviously focus my attention on the front of the line where I belong. I spot the same short, Native Indian, woman who was standing ahead of me before the rude lady cut in front of me. The short native woman is just about to order her sugar-dog.

This makes no sense.

Where is the rude lady?

I look around the busy city a second time, sifting angrily through hordes of pedestrians in search of her but the skinny woman is still nowhere to be found. Why did she cut in front of me if she never wanted a sugar-dog in the first place? I shake my head in frustration and then exit the line and begin walking unhappily to work.

I can hear and feel the crazy man following behind me.

I begin to walk faster.

I hear the speed of his footsteps increase and before I know it I can practically feel him breathing down my neck.

"Why are you rushing to a job that you hate?" He asks.

I stop abruptly.

Before I can turn around and give him a piece of my mind he crashes into me. The weight and force of his large, moving, body throws me forward but he reaches out, catching me before I fall to the ground.

I wrench myself free from his grip and turn to face him, "Don't you ever," I yell. "Put your hands on me. You don't know me and you have no right to touch me. Who do you think you are?"

"I was only trying to help. You were going to fall."

"Because you pushed me."

"I bumped into you."

I shake my head and sigh, "why in the world is this happening to me? What did I do wrong?" I mumble under my breath.

"I understand how you feel, I remember working a job I hated," he laughs. "I used to work at a call centre for a bank as a *client care representative*. It was the worst job of my life. At one point I thought I would be trapped working there forever," he shudders, his face filling with angst. "Anyhow, enough reminiscing, can you please call Ken and let him know that you hate your job and that you won't be coming into work today?"

"How do you know where I work?"

"Really?" he asks, his eyes growing large with shock.

I stare at him perplexed, waiting for an explanation.

"I would be a pretty horrible follower if I didn't know something as basic as that," he smiles.

I snap, "Don't you have anything better to do than stalk-"

"Follow," he corrects. "I'm following you."

"I don't care what you call it!" I yell. "I want it to stop or I'll call the police and have you arrested."

"Have me arrested?" he says with a pretentious little laugh. "What would you have me arrested for? I'm not doing anything wrong."

"You're not doing anything wrong? You pushed me in my back and you're following me."

"I didn't push you, I bumped into you by accident and that was mainly because you stopped walking so abruptly. You and I are equally accountable and therefore equally liable for any pain and suffering that the other party may have sustained due to this incident."

I stare at him, my lips pursed as I contemplate his words. His voice is so professional and the words flow effortlessly off of his tongue that I don't know if I should believe him or not.

"Besides," he continues. "In Canada it is not illegal to follow someone around, so I can follow you all day if I choose."

I try to think of a response but my mind is blank, could it really be legal to stalk someone in Canada?

He looks intently into my eyes, staring into my confusion before scoffing and saying, "Wow, you have no idea what is going on here, do you Vanessa?"

A cold sensation avalanches down my spine.

In a panic, I step back from the stranger as fast as my feet will allow.

"How do you know my name?" I say quickly.

He grins a devilish grin before stepping towards me, "like I said, I've been following you. I know everything I need to know about you, Vanessa. Now, let me tell you a couple of things about me. I'm not afraid of the police or any human to be frank, so you can threaten me all you want but that won't stop me. I came here today to have lunch with you and I'm not leaving here until we have lunch, Vanessa. So... now that that's out of the way are you ready to go eat?"

There is no doubt in my mind that the stranger is completely insane and needs to be locked in a white room with foam-padded walls. And there is no doubt in my mind that I should turn and run for my life or at the very least call the police and report the crazy man, but something inside of me stifles and kills my better judgment. Something within me is intrigued by his oddness and desires to know exactly who he is and why he is so interested in me because the truth is nobody has ever been interested in me. I want to see what he sees in me because I don't see anything in myself.

These are not my thoughts, these are not my thoughts, I repeat in my mind as I wrestle with my weak and lowly mother but my mother overpowers me and subdues me.

"One hour and then you will leave me alone for good?"

"Yes," he smiles.

"Fine, let's just get this over with."

"How much?"

"What?"

"How much for an hour of your time?"

"Are you serious?"

"Yes," he reaches into his pant's pocket and pulls out a chocolate brown leather wallet overflowing with bright red and light brown bills.

I think of an outrageous amount, an amount that nobody would ever be willing to pay for me.

"200 dollars," I say.

Without flinching he hands me my payment and then places his hand on his hip, creating a resting place for my arm. I glower at the opening and imagine his massive arm constricting like a hungry snake onto my wrist, cracking and devouring my bones like they were nothing more than brittle toothpicks.

"No thank you, I don't need help walking."

He chuckles and then closes the opening, placing his hand back at his side.

"Maybe I'm the one who needs help walking," he says while pretending to limp.

I scoff, "Why are you doing this? Why are you paying me for my time?"

"Because, time is far too precious not to be paid for but I think what you really want to know is why am I giving you paper money for your time."

"Exactly," I nod my head.

"Because right now that's what you believe your time is worth. If I offered you anything else you wouldn't accept it."

"What other forms of payment do you have?" I ask, slightly intrigued by his statement.

"Love, location, joy, kindness, devotion, patience, freedom, friendship, help... my house," he smiles.

"You're right, I prefer the money."

He laughs aloud.

While he and I walk to his friend's restaurant I watch him from the corner of my eyes. His facial features are soft and gentle yet chiselled and hard, one of those faces that tell other men I am a threat, I am alpha, I have killed and destroyed countless competitors to gain all that I have so don't even think about challenging me, but the same stony cruel face also tells every woman in the world that I am a protector, I am sensitive and kind, I am intimate, considerate and tender so please come and fall in love with me because the truth is I have already fallen in love with you.

Every cell in my body wants to turn away and stop gazing at him but my mother won't allow me to do so. My mother wants me to see how tall, muscular, and attractive he is, she wants me to fall head over heels in love with him.

Discretely shaking my head and throwing my mother from my thoughts I remind myself that the strange man's breathtaking good looks and perfectly polished personality was to be expected. Unattractive men did not make for good serial killers, rapists or stalkers. Unattractive men did not possess what was necessary to soothe and manipulate a random woman's heart to the point where she would willingly do anything he commanded.

Without warning the strange man stops in front of an old, rundown, clothing store. He pulls the glass door open and tries to usher me inside.

I look inside the empty store and say, "This isn't a restaurant."

"I know, Vanessa," he laughs. "I just assumed that you would like to change out of your work clothes and into something a little nicer before we go eat."

As I continue to stare into the store all of the dots begin to connect in my head- the rude lady, her sudden appearance and her suspicious disappearance, the strange man's timely arrival and the journey to his friend's restaurant that just so happens to take he and I pass an empty clothing store. The whole thing was a set-up to get me alone.

Suddenly, an image of me tied to a metal chair in a cold basement flashes through my mind.

"I'm fine with what I have on, I don't need new clothes."

"Come on Vanessa, it'll be my treat," he insists. "I know the owner and you can buy whatever you want, no strings attached."

"I said no."

"How about we go inside and look around? You may find something that you like; the clothing is beautiful and handmade."

"How many times do I have to say no?" I snap. "I don't want new clothes."

He releases the silver handle, causing the heavy glass door to slam shut.

"Please, forgive me," he says, gently bowing his head. "What you are wearing is fine, you look wonderful and my friend's restaurant is just around the corner, let's go."

"I don't want to eat at your friend's restaurant," I say while scanning Bay Street for a popular chain restaurant that has a constant flow of customers entering and exiting. "I want to go there," I point sternly.

"There!" he exclaims, his face contorting in horror. "The food there is horrible. Please, let's just go to my friends restaurant you'll love the food and the atmosphere, I promise."

"It's there," I point again. "Or no where."

CHAPTER 6

HAPPINESS

(Vanessa)

In the deepest regions of your soul you know what will make you truly happy. The hard part is accepting the fact that you may have to journey through great sadness before you can arrive at great joy.

-

"Those who sow in tears shall reap in joy."

Psalms: 126:5

****

A small glass bulb, with a thin white candle sitting inside of it, hangs luminously above the table that my stalker and I sit at. The bulb releases just enough light to ensure that both of our faces along with our meals are visible. The table-top is made of dark marble and the chairs are solid oak, cushioned with soft red leather. Subtle jazz music is playing almost inaudibly in the background and all around us men and women are laughing and conversing.

As I chew my steak, I can feel his strong gaze piercing and analysing me in a crude attempt to understand and neatly label all of the pieces that make me who I am so for him I become a whole new woman. Normally, I don't cut my meat into small perfect squares but for him I do. Normally, I don't drink my juice in small eloquent sips, inhaling sophisticatedly after each swallow, but for him I do. I do all of these things because I know that I can only get rid of a stalker by proving to him that I am not the type of woman that he thinks I am

He finally stops looking at me.

I continue looking at him.

With his fork he tears into a large piece of Atlantic Salmon, puts the pink fish in his mouth and chews on it in the most pretentious way I have ever seen a human being chew.

I take an extremely dignified sip of my royal purple juice. As the carbonated grape flavoured liquid flows down my throat I realize how ridiculous I look, I should have ordered something more refined, like red wine.

"Vanessa," he calls out to me after swallowing a mouthful of fish. "If you're unhappy with your life why don't you change your life?"

He asks the question as though he believes changing ones' life is just as simple as changing ones' clothes.

"I am happy, very happy actually," I say before taking another sip from my wine glass of purple water.

"No, you're not."

"Yes, I am," I say, fighting with myself to stay calm.

He exhales and shakes his head, "You think I'm dangerous and crazy, and you think I might harm you, correct?"

"Correct."

He smiles, "Think about that Vanessa, you are sitting in a dimly lit restaurant with a lunatic who you believe wants to hurt you. I don't think a person who is happy with their life would put their life at risk by entertaining a lunatic."

I want to storm out the restaurant but storming out will only validate his opinion of me and encourage him to chase me. I have to stand my ground, I have to fight back and prove to him that everything he thinks about me is incorrect. I need to think of something smart and hurtful to say to him, something that will rattle his confidence and give me the upper hand.

I look him over quickly.

I got it!

He is eating three large pieces of baked Salmon, green beans, diced carrots, broccoli, lentils and cauliflower.

Gluttony?

No, gluttony won't work because men enjoy being pigs.

I got it!

The waitress offered him juice or tea but he ordered a lukewarm glass of water with a slice of lemon in it.

He's cheap, he's poor.

I remember back to the supermarket and the 200 dollars now folded in my pocket.

I keep searching, seeking an imperfection that can be turned into an insecurity.

Think, think, think Vanessa.

He doesn't have a wedding ring on.

Wait a minute... he doesn't have a wedding ring on and he stalks women and pays them to spend time with him.

"You're in your late twenties or early thirties and you're not married. You spend your days following women around and paying them to spend time with you. Based on your actions you're obviously an obsessive, desperate, and controlling man who feels emasculated in some way."

He shrugs his shoulders and takes a sip of his lemon water, "That's my point Vanessa, if I am all of those things then why are you entertaining me at all? Why are you sitting here with a crazy, sociopathic, unmarried, over compensating, womanizer, and woman follower/stalker like myself?"

I shake my head, everything in me screams get up and run far away, call the police but my mother whispers in my ears and anchors me to my seat.

'Don't you dare be rude to this nice man,' my mother commands. *'He brought you out to eat at this fancy restaurant and he gave you lots of money now be smart and give him whatever he wants. The world is a rough place and a woman needs a man to take care of her and protect her.'*

I've had enough; I refuse to allow my mother's archaic, female denigrating, philosophies to rule any aspect of my life. Standing to my feet I grab my belongings and excuse myself from the table.

"Where are we going now?" he asks, mimicking me and standing to his feet. "We have twenty minutes left together."

"We're not going anywhere, I'm leaving."

"But my hour isn't up yet."

"Stay away from me you disgusting creep!" I scream, taking out the two hundred dollars from my pocket and throwing it on the table. "There! There is your money, now leave me alone!"

I can feel the eyes of everyone in the restaurant glaring in my direction. I can hear them murmuring and laughing.

"Hey buddy couldn't you find a prettier prostitute?" a man yells.

The restaurant erupts with laughter.

I freeze up, every part of me stiff with embarrassment.

I want to crawl under a rock and die.

"Vanessa, ignore them."

"Did you pay by the pound for that piece of meat?" the man attacks again with shark like precision, drawing even more blood than before.

My stalker clenches his fists, turns in the man's direction and growls, "If you say another disrespectful word to her, I promise you that you will not be able to speak for the rest of the month."

The man and the entire restaurant full of patrons fall silent.

"Vanessa," my stalker continues while staring into my eyes. "Let's leave, let's get out of here. We will finish our time together elsewhere and then I will leave you alone. I know a beautiful path by the Lakeshore, we can go for a walk," he smiles.

"Sir is everything alright? Is this woman disturbing you?"

I glance to my right. There is a young, beautiful, female waitress standing there with her hands folded. She is wearing a sleeveless, skin-tight, all black knee-high dress. She is my height with glowing skin, thick lips, thick hips, and a slim waist.

She completely ignores me and focuses all of her attention on my stalker.

I look at him.

He is wearing a nice blue suit and he looks like money.

I look at myself.

I am wearing dirty jeans and a dirty shirt and I look like trash.

I guess I would ignore me too.

My stalker looks me in my eyes and says, "No, I think I may actually be the one who is disturbing her. Vanessa, I'm sorry, please forgive me. I will leave you alone."

He reaches into his back pocket and pulls out his wallet. From it he withdraws two red fifty-dollar bills, puts the money on the table next to my two-hundred-dollars before walking out of the restaurant.

The waitress picks up all the money, clears the table and walks off without saying a word to me.

"Now that your pimp is gone," a man screams out. "Who is going to save you?"

I rush out the restaurant, my head down and my left hand covering my entire face.

CHAPTER 7

SADNESS
(Vanessa)

Sometimes our deepest sorrows turn out to be the broken, mangled, bridges that carry us to our greatest joys. When everything around you is falling apart and the earth beneath your feet feels like quicksand, you must never stop believing that things can change and that with just a few more faith filled steps your life can and will get better.

"Remember not the former things, nor consider the things of old. Behold, I am doing a new thing; now it springs forth, do you not perceive it? I will make a way in the wilderness and rivers in the desert."

Isaiah 43:18-19
****

Summer finishes without another incident, fall begins and ends without disturbance and winter comes and goes quickly. And just like the white, cold, snow that blanketed the earth all of my thoughts surrounding my dreaded stalker melt then evaporate bit by bit until finally, he is gone from my mind for good and my life is back to normal.

*

A loud gust of wind causes the heavy spring rain to crash forcefully against my room window. It is eight in the morning but the sky is as black as night and filled with large dark clouds and sudden thick flashes of lightning. Today, I want to call in sick from work, I want to cover myself with a sea of sheets and sleep for the entire day but I have used up all of my sick days and if I attempt to call in sick I know without a doubt that my evil boss Ken will fire me. I hate my job but I need my job, so driven by the same ugly truth that pushes every minimum waged employee to leave his or her warm bed and head to a job that he or she hates I get dressed and go outside to stand in the rain and wait for my bus.

I arrive to work thirty minutes late but this morning it was not my fault. My car was stolen again, and to make matters worse, a short teenaged girl with bright pink hair tried to sneak on the back of the bus without paying. The bus driver, an equally short man sporting a bright red turban and a thick black beard, refused to drive the bus until the child paid her fare or exited the bus. The whole incident went on for fifteen minutes until the teenager, at the command and violent roar of all the other passengers, finally exited the bus but not before hurling profanities at the driver and proudly displaying her middle finger to the entire bus.

Ken is standing by the front door when I unwillingly drag my wet body into his Fish Emporium.

"Nessy," Ken says, shaking his head as soon as he notices me. "Come and see me at the beginning of your first break. The beginning Nessy, not the end, the beginning... you and I need to have a very serious talk about your performance."

Today, Ken stinks of frankincense and has adorned himself with a silver chain and a gold crucifix. I love the story of the crucifix. God supposedly came down from heaven and tried to further enslave humans with more philosophies and rules, but we humans said no thank you and then we tortured him, mocked him, spit on him, nailed him to a cross and proudly displayed his battered and bruised body before sticking a cold iron spear in his side and sending him back to his imaginary kingdom in the sky. Now humans wear crosses and put them on top of tall, beautiful, buildings in order to remind god what will happen to him if he ever tries to come back to earth.

"Vanessa!"

I stumble from my thoughts and back into Ken's supermarket.

"Yes Ken," I answer abruptly.

"I said come to my office right at the beginning of your first break, not the end. Do you understand?"

"Yes Ken, yes I understand."

"Then respond, Nessy. If you understand then you respond, you show understanding through response. You tulala," he says, shaking his head and grunting loudly before storming off.

Tulala means idiot in his language, he probably thinks I don't know what it means but I have the Internet and Google. I am not a tulala if anything he is the tulala. I have been stealing pieces of salmon for the last year and he has no idea... tulala.

I walk to the back of the store, take off my raincoat, put on my apron, pick up my knife, and enter my fridge. When I finish my first shipment of fish I take my first break.

"At the beginning of your break not the end," I mimic Ken as I run to the convenient store across the street to purchase a pack of Twinkies.

Ken is not allowed to tell me what to do with my breaks I think to myself as I slowly chew each pastry, taking my time to savour my cream filled treats.

Ken isn't boss of my breaks.

I can do whatever I want on my breaks.

Three minutes before the end of my break I walk slowly down the dimly lit corridor and enter Ken's office exactly as my break ends... if he needs to speak with me he can speak to me on his time, not mine.

I sit down on a dirty red, leather, chair and stare at Ken.

My right eye begins to twitch sporadically.

"Nessy, you're fired," Ken says, his face and voice void of all emotion. "I'll pay you for the rest of your shift but I want you to leave right now."

"But-"

"No buts Nessy," he cuts in. "You are always late or calling in sick. I pay you to show up when you're scheduled to show up not only when you feel like showing up."

"Please Ken," I beg. "I need this job. I'll do better I swear. I'll never be late again; I'll never call in sick again. I was late today because the bus, the girl with pink hair," I sob. "My car-"

"Enough! Enough excuses, Nessy!" Ken yells. "I don't care what you do or what happens to you when you're not at work, but the moment that your shift starts I expect you to be in the back of my store doing your job."

"I know Ken, you're right, I'm wrong, I'm such a tulala, I'm sorry and I swear it will never happen again."

"If I'm right and you're wrong then why are you still here, Nessy?" He asks coldly. "I am done discussing this, now please leave."

I exit Ken's office, walk to the back room, hang up my apron for the final time and collect my belongings. Movies, books and music always claim that the path to happiness can only be travelled when one is being directed by one's heart, but the truth is the heart is misguided. The heart is a crazy schizophrenic lunatic who has no idea what it wants. My heart pestered me for years, begging me to quit my job and now that I'm no longer working for Ken my heart is telling me to beg for my job back. It tells me that it misses the solace and surety of Ken's captivity. It tells me that we will suffer and die of starvation without Ken. My heart that was once so bold and courageous is now weak and feeble.

***

When I enter my apartment I hear them scattering all around me. I want to scream at them and tell them that I don't care about them, that they are unimportant and dirty but I am too tired and frustrated to scream. I head straight to my room, fall onto my mattress, drown myself in pillows and lay there until sleep comes and whisks me away.

Later that evening my phone rings, waking me.

I pick up.

"I'm so sorry Angel, the devil was in my brain but he's gone now. You can come back, now, he's gone."

I hang up the phone and go back to sleep.

Hours later when the sun can no longer be seen in the sky I slog into my shower and scrub away dry fish scales from my skin and hair. As I watch fish scales stream from my body and run down the drain, I realize that I'm broke in more ways than one.

Without warning I collapse to my knees and begin to weep aloud. I cry until it hurts inside of my chest, I cry until I can no longer feel tears flowing from my bloodshot eyes. I cry until the pain within me swells over and suffocates my open mouth wale, causing only the sound of water crashing against worn bath tiles to be heard.

'*Just give up,*' a subtle thought rises in my mind. '*Clog your bathtub, let the water run until the tub is full, and then lie down and rest. It will all be over soon and then you will be happy.*'

I search the small, cramped, tub for my rubber water stopper but I'm unable to find it.

'*Don't give up, don't give up, keep searching, don't give up.*'

I grab my washrag and stuff it securely into the drain then laydown and wait. Fifteen agonizing minutes of life pass but my bathtub still isn't full of water.

I stagger to my feet.

Turn off the pipe.

Pick up my useless rag.

Pull my shower curtains to one side, wrap myself with a white towel, and exit the washroom. The underwear that I put on squeezes my thighs, my pants refuse to button, and my bra strap cuts into my skin like a single thread of barbwire.

Nothing fits.

Nothing fits because I don't belong here!

I finish getting dressed as best as I can and then I lie in my bed.

My phone rings.

I know it's him so I ignore it.

My phone rings once again.

I ignore it.

There is a loud knock on my front door.

I don't know who it is so I ignore it.

There is another knock on my door, a heavy-handed thud that demands my attention.

I answer the door.

My landlord, David Kcaplan, is standing in the hallway staring at me. Kcaplan is a tall, chubby man who speaks with a thick Russian brogue. Today, he is wearing washed out jeans, a black t-shirt with white paint marks on it and steel toe work boots. David always looks as if he has just finished repairing something or working hard even though he never does any work at all. The toilet in my washroom hasn't flushed correctly for the past two weeks and he still hasn't gotten around to repairing it.

"What is it David?"

"You have to leave, Vanessa. This is notice for your eviction. Take it."

My heart drops to my stomach.

"Your neighbours complain," he continues.

"About what?" The question coils from my trembling lips.

"About you, about how you live."

"There is nothing wrong with how I live."

He tilts his head to the side, looking into my apartment.

"Listen," I defend myself before he can attack. "The condition of my apartment shouldn't affect anybody else in this building. They're not living with me and they sure as heck don't pay my rent. You can tell them to go-"

"This, this is why they complain. You see this?" David breaks in, stomping his discoloured brown boots on a large black cockroach that was attempting to escape my apartment.

"That cockroach could have come from anywhere," I snap. "There were cockroaches in the building when I moved in."

"You have two weeks," He says before handing me the pink notice and walking off.

I close my front door.

My heart is beating out of control.

I try to read the notice but my eyes are blurry with tears. I lean against my wall and try to calm myself down, I just need some time to rest and think but this world won't let me have a single minute of peace. This world is always attacking me, always hitting me when I'm not looking!

Suddenly, I feel something shatter within me causing everything around me to become valueless. The pink paper becomes confetti in my hands. Loud, burdened, footsteps and heavy grunts fill my ears as I storm into my tiny kitchen. Pulling my top drawer open I grab the sharpest knife I can find and point the cold silver blade at my heart.

CHAPTER 8

BIBLE

(Vanessa)

Some people hate the bible because of what others have said. Some people love the bible because of what others have said. Read it for yourself and come to a conclusion.

''All Scripture is given by inspiration of God, and is profitable for doctrine, for reproof, for correction, for instruction in righteousness, that the man of God may be complete, thoroughly equipped for every good work'.'

2 Timothy 3:16-17
****

At last, at last, I'm free!
I finally did it.
I finally killed myself.
I don't know where I am or what exactly I am but I seem to be formless and floating peacefully in a warm pool of endless blackness. I want to cry tears of happiness and jump for joy but I don't think my new state has the ability to cry or jump. I try desperately to form an image of myself but there is nothing around me to mirror my image. Awareness of one's self is reliant on observations of one's environment, and the objects and beings that inhabit that environment, but when you are floating in an infinite pool of extreme blackness it is impossible to observe and therefore impossible to know one's self.
Using what I believe can be considered my mind, I will myself to move and experience something more than this all-consuming pool of darkness.
Nothing happens.
I concentrate harder, using the full force of mind to create some form of light.
Nothing happens.

Light is visually perceived radiant energy, I remember my physics teacher saying, but then again that is a human definition of light. I am no longer a human, I no longer perceive the way in which humans perceive and I therefore must rework my understanding of all things, I must empty myself of my humanity if I desire to be the new me.

As I am draining myself of my humanity, vigorously erasing all earthly thoughts, concepts and feelings the sudden heavy drawl of a man's voice breaks through the silence and darkness that surrounds me. Instantly, tears pour from my two eyes and the crude body, and sad life that I thought I had escaped rematerializes. A small light flicks on freeing me from my sea of night only to reveal the cruel face of my stalker.

He smiles at me.

I scream as loud as I can.

The entire room floods with surging white light.

A tall Chinese woman, wearing blue scrubs, is walking quickly towards me.

"Are you ok ma'am?" she asks while quickly analysing me for any visible afflictions. "Are you feeling pain?"

I stare at the woman and then rapidly move my eyes around the now lit room. There is a television to my left, a sink to my right, blue walls all around me, and an open window surrounded by soft peach coloured curtains.

"Where... where am I?"

"You're in Toronto Western hospital, ma'am."

I look around the room a second time and then inhale the dull fragrance of sanitation that only a hospital could manufacture.

"Why am I here, why can't I move?"

"You had a mild heart attack. You'll begin to regain control of your limbs in a few hours or so ma'am, but for now please just relax and rest," she says. "I have to finish my rounds, but I'll be back later to check-up on you. If you need anything you can have your husband press the big red button at the side of your bed."

The nurse rushes out of the room before I can correct her wildly incorrect statement.

"How are you feeling, Vanessa?" My stalker asks.

"You promised me that you would leave me alone, you gave me your word."

"I did leave you alone. Your Landlord found my business card in your apartment and he called me and told me that you were in the hospital, so I rushed over. I just wanted to make sure that you were all right."

My stalker's story causes me to feel vulnerable and uneasy. I imagine David standing over my sprawled out body with the knife lying next to me. I wonder if David realized that I was trying to kill myself, I wonder if he told my stalker.

I stare into my stalker's brown eyes, trying desperately to figure out what he knows. He doesn't seem to know anything... but I'm not certain.

"I'm fine," I respond. "So you can leave now."

"Vanessa," he says my name softly. "I came all this way to ensure that you were okay, I'd like to spend a little time with you if you don't mind. Allow me to have two hours of your time, please."

I sneer at him.

He smiles at me.

I'm onto him.

His plan of attack is so ridiculously juvenile, so simple minded, and blatantly obvious that I can't believe I didn't notice it sooner. First it was one minute, then it was one hour, and now it is two hours. He's trying to normalize the strangeness of his presence by subtly increasing the amount of time he and I spend together.

"I do mind," I say firmly. "I want you to leave, right now."

"Understood."

He stands to his feet, grabs his bright yellow raincoat and walks casually towards the room door. Inches from the door, inches from my peace of mind, he stops abruptly, reaches into his oversized yellow pockets and pulls out something pink and small.

He turns back around and faces me.

"I almost forgot to give you this," he says holding the item high in the air as he walks back towards my bed.

My eyebrows furrow as the object becomes clearer, the closer he gets.

"Where did you get that from?" I snap.

"From an elderly gentleman who was here visiting you earlier. He refused to tell me his name but said that you would know who he was just by seeing this."

"Throw that thing away," I grimace, my voice hot with anger.

"Pardon?"

"Throw that thing in the garbage and then get out!" I yell.

"The garbage?"

"Yes, the garbage, and then get out."

"This is a very good book though," he says calmly while staring intently at the pink, timeworn, bible that I used to own as a child.

"There is nothing good about that book, it promotes hypocrisy and evil, then uses the man in the sky excuse to justify those evils. That book is the worst book in the world."

"What is the man in the sky excuse?"

"The nonsensical belief that evil and good are fleeting ideals that are based only on the schizophrenic desires of some all powerful man in the sky. Evil is evil unless the crazy man in the sky says that evil is good, good is good unless the crazy man in the sky says that good is evil, and the crazy man in the sky is always changing his crazy mind, he is always commanding humans to do contradictory things. That book makes an unstable, imaginary, thing the anchoring force of mankind's morality and the validating force of mankind's depravity."

"Really?" he says opening the small, pink, book and flipping through its worn, white pages. "If you don't mind, can you give me an example, please?"

"I can give you hundreds."

"One will suffice," he chuckles.

"And then you'll leave?"

"Yes," he smiles.

I roll my eyes in disdain, "In the book of Judges, Chapter 21, the man in the sky condones kidnapping and rape. God's so called chosen people abducted 200 women and forced those women into marriage, yet nobody sees that as evil because it is in the bible and because god said to do it."

I pause for a moment and try to catch my breath but it eludes me.

"Abraham is another perfect example," I struggle to continue. "Abraham was going to kill his son because god commanded him to do it. If something like that happened today everybody would call Abraham crazy, throw him in a nuthouse, and Child Protective Services would put his son in a foster home. But because god commanded Abraham to do it, and because it is written in the bible, all of a sudden sacrificing children is a good thing, and now billions of foolish people love *Abraham*. Jews, Muslims, and Christians all want to be the children of a man who attempted to murder his own child. Does that make any sen-" I stop speaking abruptly, my heart is palpitating and I can't catch my breath at all.

I glance over at my stalker.

"Are you ok, Vanessa? Should I press the red button?"

I take a deep breath, a tiny bit of oxygen enters my mouth and squeezes, painfully, down my lungs.

"Vanessa?"

"I'm fine... I... I just need... to catch my breath," I struggle.

"I'm going to press the red button," he declares.

"Don't... you... dare... touch... that button!" I try to yell. "I... said... I'm... fine."

"Fine," he says sternly, his eyes firm and unrelenting. "You have literally ten seconds to catch your breath and then after that I don't care what you say... I'm pressing the button and getting a nurse in here."

Twelve seconds later I'm breathing somewhat normally and my stalker is back sitting in the little chair at my bedside.

"I've given you your example and now I want you to leave," I say, my voice still slightly laboured.

"Are you joking? You were just having trouble breathing, Vanessa. I'm not going to just leave you here by yourself. What if you die?"

"If I live or die has nothing to do with you, we're not friends. You said if I gave you an example you would leave, now leave."

"Okay, okay, fine I'll leave but before I go do you mind if I at least respond to your examples?"

"Fine," I answer sharply. "I'm actually interested in hearing how anybody could defend the murdering of children and the abduction of women."

"Great," he smiles arrogantly. "So, to begin, God didn't command or desire the 200 men of the tribe of Benjamin to abduct the 200 daughters of Israel. The Israelites of that time, like every other nation past and present, had freewill and used their freewill to resist God's will. Just because the Israelites were God's chosen people doesn't mean that they were perfect people or that God supported all of their decisions. In fact God was often upset with the Israelites for their disobedience and reprobate ways. But that in of itself is the beauty of the bible, it shows us horrors and evils that disgusts us and makes us sick to our core and then it shows us a Holy, Perfect, God Who is willing to love and help humanity rise above our depravity. The bible isn't about God leading mankind to evil the bible is about God turning things around, it is about God turning mankind from **evil** so that we can **live,"** he laughs. "Did you see what I did there, I used the words turn around and then I turned around the word evil so that it-"

"What about Abraham?" I interrupt with a scoff.

"What Abraham did was not evil or a contradiction, it was an expression of unwavering faith to a God who had never lied to or failed Abraham. God promised Abraham that his barren wife, Sara, would conceive a son and that son would give rise to a great nation, a nation that would outnumber the stars in the sky. That promised son was Isaac, so when God told Abraham to kill Isaac Abraham remembered God's promise and trusted that God would not... In fact Abraham knew that God could not break His word because it is impossible for God to lie. Abraham understood that the moment that God promises or says something that thing immediately forms into spiritual matter and eventually becomes physical matter, which meant that Isaac could not die and remain dead until he had children.

To Abraham God was the epitome of life. God had created and animated every single thing in the universe, so Abraham trusted that if his son did happen to die then God would reanimate him in almost the same way that we would put a discharged battery back into a lifeless cell phone," he laughs. "Life is something that is physical and tangible to God, knowing this is what allowed Abraham to do what he did."

"Can you leave now?"

"Huh?"

"Leave," I enunciate. "I want you to leave. I don't want to hear why you believe in some crazy man in the sky, just leave."

"Oh...okay," he laughs. "You sure you don't want to maybe talk a little longer? I have nothing of importance to do for the rest of the day.... To be honest with you, if I go home I'm most likely just going to sit on my couch and wish I were still here speaking with you so I might as well just stay here," he laughs again.

I shoot him a stern stare.

"I'll leave right now," he laughs. "But, if you don't want this," he waves my old pink bible in front of my face. "Do you mind if I take it home with me? I know someone who would love it. She loves anything pink and sparkly."

"You can do whatever you want with that thing just don't leave it in this room unless it's in the garbage."

He nods his head and then exits the hospital room.

'He's wonderful, you should marry him and have some babies,' my mother says.

'He's crazy, don't trust him, stay far away from him,' my mind says.

CHAPTER 9

PERFECTION
(Vanessa)

Love is most present when we strip ourselves of all selfish standards.

-

Love is patient and kind; love does not envy or boast; it is not arrogant or rude. It does not insist on its own way; it is not irritable or resentful; it does not rejoice at wrongdoing, but rejoices with the truth. **Love bears all things, believes all things, hopes all things, and endures all things.**

1 Corinthians 13:4-7
****

The next morning, when I have regained some control of my body, I free myself from bed and explore the hospital. Walking up and down grey hallway after grey hallway, I eventually find myself standing before a large window that overlooks an endless forest of skyscrapers. There are no trees, no blades of grass, and no wild animals as far as the eye can see. In order for these massive buildings of curved glass, bent steel, and chiselled stone to have been constructed something had to be destroyed, something had to be killed. My life was no different, my whole life I have been wounded and misused so that others could manifest their desires and construct their dreams atop my pain.

In all of my life I have never harmed a single person and yet here I am, standing by myself in the empty entrails of a drab hospital trying to recover from the merciless attacks of others. The people who hurt me are still out there enjoying life; they are walking around free and happy meanwhile I am suffering. I hate them but a large part of me wants to be just like them, even though I know it is wrong apart of me wants to stop being a victim and start being an attacker. It would be so sweet and satisfying to manipulate others so that I could take advantage of their pain and ignorance. I think about my stalker with his fancy clothes and his gold jewellery, I should bleed him dry for every dollar he owns.

A woman screams, her shrilled cry echoes ghost like in the empty hallway and sends a cold chill down my spine. A short man, with thick black hair, storms past me. Stopping meters from where I am standing the man clenches both his fists and begins to pound them against the hard hospital walls before crumbling to his knees.

"Please, God!" He cries out. "Please, save him, spare his life. I need him, God. I need him to live."

I step closer.

"You win!" he screams. "I'll do whatever you want, I'll be a good person just please don't do this to me. Not again! Please, not again. God, please, you have to save him!"

I turn from the man and walk inconspicuously to the room that both the man and the scream emerged from.

I peek inside.

A tiny, wheat-skinned, woman with long messy hair sits on a large white bed. The woman is sobbing and sweating profusely as she rocks back and forth. There are nurses, in purple scrubs, surrounding the woman's bed but the nurses are standing like department store mannequins, powerless to do anything about the lifeless baby in the woman's hands.

The wheat-skinned woman releases another blood-curdling cry but this time a series of tears are wrenched from my eyes. I understand her pain; the pain of giving birth to death, the pain of having high expectations but receiving low results, the unbearable pain of failing at producing a new and better life... I understand. My heart pangs me and oceans of tears begin to roll from my eyes. I wish her pain would go away. I'm sad that her baby is dead; no person should have to hold their dead child in their arms.

"Vanessa!" Someone screams my name from behind me.

When I turn around the most annoying man in the universe is walking towards me with an ear-to-ear smile painted on his face and large bouquet of flowers in his right hand. His long hair is wrapped in a tall bright yellow turban that sits high on his head like an ugly beehive. He is wearing low-cut light

brown leather boots, fitted dark blue jeans and a blinding white dress-shirt along with a silver watch.
I wipe my face clean of all liquids then grunt loudly, unapologetically displaying my annoyance.
"What the heck is wrong with you?! Why won't you just leave me-"
"Hold onto that thought," he interrupts before rudely handing me the pile of flowers and continuing towards the short man with the thick black hair.
I want to throw the colourful bouquet of flowers onto the floor and step all over them but knowing him he would most certainly leave and return with more flowers so for that reason and that reason alone, I cradle the flowers in my arms... they smell amazing.
"Sir, are you okay? What happened?" My stalker asks, sitting on the dirty hospital floor alongside the man.
"I give up," the man cries, his voice laboured with a heavy, crippling, grief. "I'm done, this was the last straw. This was her last chance."
"What happened?" my stalker asks again.
"My wife can't..." he sighs. "She can't have normal children, something is wrong with her. Our son is... Our son is dead because of her and our daughter; our daughter has Down syndrome because of her. This baby was supposed to be normal," the man begins to sob uncontrollably. "The Doctor promised me that this baby would be normal. I did all of the tests and I followed all of the rules. I made sure that my wife only ate healthy, organic, foods and took her daily vitamins and came for bi-weekly check-ups. I plugged out the microwave and took three months off from work just so that I could be at home to assist her with everything. I treated her like a queen and she does this to me," the man yells. "I did every thing right. He was supposed to be normal," the man inhales deeply as more tears stream like powerful, unforgiving, rivers down his cheeks. "I deserve a normal child, a normal family, a normal life but she can't give that to me. I love my wife, I really love her but," he exhales. "I made a mistake. I made a big, big, mistake," he says solemnly. "She isn't the right woman for me, I should have never married her. I deserve a woman who can give me normal children, just one

normal child," he sobs. "Just one."

"I'm deeply sorry for your loss, sir," my stalker sighs while slowly shaking his head and placing his right hand on the short man's shoulder. "I know how it feels to lose someone you love, to have expectations and not have those expectations materialize but nonetheless you shouldn't be out here. You have no right to be out here."

I gasp in entertained horror at the abrasiveness of my stalker's words, at his total disregard for the pain that the crying man is currently suffering through.

Slowly, the man raises his head, looks up and stares into the eyes of my stalker. He opens his mouth to speak but his pain overwhelms him and muffles his words.

"I don't know why you and your wife have been unable to give birth to the *type* of child that you want and that you feel you deserve," my stalker continues. "But I do know that it is not your wife's fault or something that she is doing on purpose. Your wife is not broken and your daughter is not a mistake. Too often, we men create in our heads this ludicrous image of what we consider to be the perfect life, the perfect family, the perfect woman and then we hurt, misuse, disregard, and refuse to love anyone that does not meet our foolish standards of perfection, but sometimes God gives us the people we need, not the people we want. Your son, a quote unquote normal child, is not what you need at this very moment. Right now your current wife and your current daughter are what you need and they are also what you should want. They deserve to experience the fullness of your love. Your family deserves to know and feel that they are perfect in your eyes and a husband should never be absent from his wife when she is in pain. You and her are one flesh and need to be by each other's side no matter what. If you need to cry, cry in there with her, if you need to mourn and breakdown then mourn and breakdown in there with her, whatsoever you need to do, do it in there with her."

The short man sobs, "You're right, you're right but... but I don't know what to say to her. I'm just so unhappy and I've... I've treated her so horribly and I don't want to hurt her, I love her but I'm not happy. I want what I want. I want a normal child."

"Don't allow your standards to cause the people around you to feel low and mistreated. The first standard that any person should have is respect and love for those around them."

"What... what do I say to her?"

"What is in your heart to say to her?"

"Nothing good, my heart is full of anger, hate," the man sniffles, pulling liquid back into his nose. "And hurt."

"Then say nothing, just go in there and be there for her, be silent until the right words come and then speak light into her darkness and healing into her pain but for now just go in there and hold her and allow her to hold you."

My stalker helps the broken man to his feet and together they walk towards the room housing his broken wife and dead child.

I move away from the room door.

My stalker nods his head at me and mouths the words *thank you,* before telling the man his name and handing him one of his fake business cards. The short man hugs Shariffe and thanks him before walking back into the hospital room and nestling beside his wife... together they cry, mourning the precocious loss of their child.

"Alright," Shariffe smiles. "Let's get you back into bed and get those flowers in some water."

"Why are you here?"

"I forgot to bring you a gift yesterday so I came today to deliver those flowers to you. But we have to place them in water before they begin to dry up."

He takes the bouquet from my hands and walks down the hall towards my room.

I know exactly what he's trying to do.

He's trying to control me by making his commands seem like soft suggestions that will contribute to my overall well-being. I'm not an idiot; everything he is doing is basic psychology. Every human wants to be happy and when someone is able to convince you that what he or she says and does to you will make your life better and bring you happiness, you will do whatever he or she commands you to do without question. The desire to be happy is everyone's weakness.

Refusing to be controlled, I turn around and begin to walk in the opposite direction of my stalker. After almost an hour's worth of walking, my feet and thighs are sore, and I am tired of hearing people scream and seeing withering bodies tethered to transparent feeding tubes. When I arrive back at my room all of the lights are on, the flowers are in a large glass jug that is half empty with water and Shariffe is nowhere to be found.

I exhale happily, enter my room, take off my slippers, and get right into bed. Minutes later, as I'm about to fall asleep, I hear the toilet in my washroom flush.

I sit up.

The washroom door opens and Shariffe emerges.

He sits on the small chair beside my bed, "I got you a card to go along with the flowers, do you mind if I read it to you?"

Sighing, I say, "Do whatever you want because nothing I say seems to matter to you."

He rips open the light blue envelope, excitedly pulls out a colourful card and begins to read, "To my wonderful friend Vanessa. Get well soon."

He closes the card.

That's it? I think to myself. That's what you wanted to read to me? Eight words...

"What do you think? Do you like it? It took me all night to write it."

I look at him to see if he is joking but I can see it on his face that he is serious, that he believes the words that he just read to me are memorable in some way.

"It's...ah... nice. Thank you...?"

He smiles and hands me the card.

"I brought you one more thing," reaching his hands under the small wooden chair he withdraws a red lunch bag and pulls out a round glass container. "Its Ital soup," he smiles.

"I don't want any of your soup."

"Trust me, you will want to try this soup. I made it myself and not to brag but I'm the best cook in my house... well... I'm the only cook in my house but that is neither here nor there."

"No thank you."

"Come on Vanessa, try it."

"I said no!"

With a sigh he places the bowl back into the red bag that he took it from and then says, "How about we make a deal?

You try my soup and if you don't like it I will leave right now and never ever come back no matter what happens."

"You always say you'll never come back but you always come back," I shoot back.

"I mean it this time, if you do not like my soup you will never see me again. I promise."

"And if I do like it?"

"Then I'm happy and you're on the road to a quick recovery. Besides, think about it logically. The worst thing that could possibly happen to you from drinking my soup is that you die. But if you die then you won't have to put up with me anymore," he smiles an exaggerated smile causing his cheeks to flare up.

I fight to keep a serious face but can't help but release a tiny smile.

"Ok, I'll try it but you have to take the first sip, maybe I can get rid of you without putting my own life at risk."

"That's the spirit!" He pours a portion of the soup into a Styrofoam cup and drinks it. "Still alive," he jests, turning the empty cup upside down before handing me the container.

As I hold the warm glass bowl in my hands, and stare at the puke green liquid, I begin to regret my decision but nonetheless I put a small spoonful of the strange soup in my mouth and swallow. Five minutes later the bowl is completely empty and I am licking the silver spoon trying desperately to withdraw any remnants of flavour that it holds.

'He can cook!' my mother screams excitedly. *'He can cook! You should never reject a man who can cook and is willing to cook for you... but maybe he is gay, men should not know how to cook.'*

I shake my mother from mind.

Maybe it's the soup, maybe he put something in it, some kind of drug, but I feel warm and calm all over and I can't stop smiling.

Maybe its weed soup, maybe Ital means weed.

I fight with the feeling, but it overpowers and subdues me and fills me.

"What did you put in the soup?"

"Love," he smiles. "A whole lot of love."

"I'm serious," I say while smiling uncontrollably from ear-to-ear.

"Special, secret, recipe," he smiles. "It was given to me by an ageless priest who lives under the tallest tree on the highest mountain beside the deepest lake in Jamaica. He told me that I could only tell one other person the recipe and I have already told it to Candice... I'm sorry."

The warm, happy, feeling continues to move all throughout me.

"That's fine," I continue to smile. "Jamaica MON," I snort and giggle to myself. "No worries... be happy," I laugh hysterically.

"Here," he says suddenly, handing me two silver keys.

"What are these?" I can't stop smiling and giggling.

"Your Landlord called me. He told me that he evicted you and that he was going to throw your belongings in the dump if someone did not come and get them immediately. So I had a moving company place all of your belongings in storage. One key is for my front door and the other key is for the storage unit containing all of your belongings. I think now would be a really good time for you to reconsider my offer. Come home with me, Vanessa."

Instantly, the warm calm feeling that enveloped me dissolves and I regain control of myself.

"No," I snap, my face once again lathered with seriousness. "I'm not going home with you. I told you that already."

"But," he stares at me with a confused look in his eyes. "You have nowhere else to go. I'm your only option."

His words hit me hard, smashing into me over and over again, as I repeat them in my head.

"Life is interesting," he says while staring at and playing with the large wooden bracelet on his wrist. "Life sometimes demands the complete destruction of all we know, all we hate and all we love before it manifests itself," he stops speaking and his eyes go wide. "I understand, I finally understand, if I want you to come home with me I have to let everything else go. Keep both keys, think about what you would like to do and then I will come back tomorrow to pick up my house key or to pick you up depending on what you decide," he says before jumping to his feet and rushing out of the room like a man who is on fire and in search of water.

I stare at the two silver keys.

My lips quiver as my eyes pool with tears.

I have no one to turn to.
I have nowhere to go.

CHAPTER 10

DECISIONS
(Vanessa)

What should you do when you don't know what to do?

"Trust in the Lord with all thine heart; and lean not unto thine own understanding. In all thy ways acknowledge him, and he shall direct thy paths. "

Proverbs 3:5-6
****

The sun has barely risen in the dark morning sky when Shariffe enters my room, turns on the light without my permission, and sits down on the small blue chair next to my bed.

"Vanessa," he whispers. "Are you awake yet?"

I keep my eyes closed and slow my breathing.

"Vanessa," he whispers a little louder. "Are you awake?"

I lie as still as humanly possible, regulating the rising and falling of my chest before turning my body and pretending to snore.

"Vanessa, I know you're faking it. I know you're awake."

I grunt, open my eyes, sit up from my bed and scream out in frustration, "What do you want? What do you want? What do you want? Why are you here? Why are you torturing my life?!"

"This is great!" he exclaims. "The soup is working."

"What?" I shake my head in confusion. "What are you talking about?"

"The Ital soup, it's working."

"How can you tell?"

"Yesterday there were two thick red veins and a small cloud of blood in your left eye but today they're gone."

Fully awakened by the strangeness of his observations, I sit up straight and stare at him.

He laughs and as if reading my mind he says, "It's called Eye-ology. God is Love so when He designed our physical and our spiritual beings He designed them for the sole purpose of giving and receiving love. We were not designed to abuse or be abused. We were never meant to feel pain or neglect so when we are not receiving or giving the love that God intended for us to receive and give our body will warn us. The eyes are just one of the many ways that our body speaks."

I scoff, "I don't believe in spirits or god or this Eye-ology thing."

"Do you mind if I study your eyes?"

"Go ahead," I laugh.

He looks deep into my eyes, studying them meticulously, "you get shooting pains in your right thigh and your left knee, usually when it rains... oh and your iron levels are low... very low."

"How'd, how did you do that?" I ask in shock.

"Lots and lots of research. But like I said earlier, your body is constantly speaking to you but it is up to you whether or not you will learn its language."

"What do the red lines in your eyes mean?"

He chuckles, "They mean that I have been up all night cleaning, shopping, and preparing for your arrival."

"My arrival?"

He nods his head.

"But I told you that I'm not going home with you."

"I know," he reaches into a blue thermal lunch bag and withdraws another bowl of his Ital Soup but this time the soup is mud brown instead of puke green.

"Then why were you preparing your home for my arrival?"

"God told me to."

I jeer and laugh sarcastically, "Let me get this straight, I exist and I told you that I'm not coming home with you. God doesn't exist and he told you that I am going home with you and you chose to listen to the thing that doesn't exist over the person that does exist?"

"God does exist," he says flatly, taking the lid off the soup bowl.

"In your head," I respond, taking the soup from his hand and beginning to spoon it into my mouth.

"No... Actually I exist in God's head. My existence is based completely on God's thoughts. God's existence is in no way dependant on my thoughts. If God doesn't think I exist then I cease to exist. It is actually very heart-warming when you really think about it; the fact that even when no human is thinking about you and you feel lonely and neglected God is thinking about you every second of every day. He is focused on you and that's why you continue to exist."

"Riiiight..."

"So, are you coming home with me?"

I sigh aloud, "Yes... I'm coming. But my choice has nothing to do with some imaginary man in the sky. Like you said yesterday, I've been evicted and have nowhere else to go. You waited and then you asked me when you knew I had no other choice but to say yes. God didn't make me say yes, my circumstances made me say yes."

"Okay."

"That's it? That's all you're going to say?"

"Yup."

I turn my head away from him and begin to breathe rhythmically, attempting to shake off the lethargy of the whole situation but it sucks onto me like a large, greedy, leech.

"Well," I fire back. "I'm not going anywhere with you unless you leave all of your information with the hospital receptionist and you have to get a police check done. For all I know you could be a serial killer or a rapist."

He laughs aloud, slaps his left knee dramatically, and jerks his body with such force that his long black dreads fly forward, covering his face.

"That was a good one, that was a really good one," he says fixing his hair so that his face is once again visible. "I haven't laughed that hard in forever, I needed that. Oh boy," he chuckles. "I really needed that, thankyou, Vanessa."

I sit stone-faced, my eyes and lips unbending like thick pieces of steal, "I'm not joking."

"Do I look like a serial killer or a rapist to you?" He turns his head from side to side.

"Serial killers and rapists don't have a specific look. You should know that if you're really a lawyer," I say.

He shakes his head and lets out a short chuckle, "if it will help to ease your mind then I will do it, let's go."

I rise from the bed, gather my clothes, and enter the washroom. As soon as the door clicks shut my inner self begins to scream at me.

'What the heck are you doing? You don't know him and you're going home with him. You're just like your mother, you're desperate and lonely and you believe that you need a man to survive.'

"I'm not like my mother," I fight back with a mumble. "He and I are going to the police station. If he has a criminal record then I won't go home with him."

'You Idiot,' my inner self screams at the top of her lungs. *'What if he kills you before you even get to the police station? What if he doesn't have a criminal record but he wants to make you his first victim?'*

"Look at all of the nice things he has done for me. Why would he go through all of this just to kill me?"

'Nice things?' My inner voice scoffs. *'You mean cheap flowers and canned soup? When you and I end up in a small metal box in his basement don't say I didn't warn you.'*

I exit the washroom fully dressed.

"You took so long in there that I thought you chickened out and flew away," he laughs.

"Chickens can't fly, you tulala," I mumble in response.

"It's a good thing they can't," he laughs.

I shake my head.

After speaking to the receptionist, we take the elevator down to the parking garage where he leads me to a rust covered car that doesn't look like it can fit the both of us comfortably. The inside of the car chauffeurs a repugnant odour that smells like a mixture of every horrible thing that I have ever had the displeasure of smelling.

Shariffe puts the key in the ignition and turns it forcefully, but nothing happens.

"Come on, come on, don't fail me now. Vanessa has finally agreed to come home with me and you have to get us there safely," he says while jiggling the key and pumping his foot on the gas pedal before turning the key again.

The old car coughs and shakes to life.

I shake my head, what did I get myself into?

***

Together, he and I walk towards the main entrance of the police station. He opens the large glass door for me, allowing me to walk in ahead of him. *'Every respectable man should hold a door open for his woman. Opening a door for a woman is a man's way of saying I put you first, I want you to rest and benefit from all of my hard work. A man who opens doors for a woman is a good man. A woman should never marry a man who doesn't open doors for her. A lady should not have to open her own doors.'*

Get out of my head mom, get out of my head mom, get out right now!

She leaves.

The police station is neat, quiet and odourless, a welcomed change from Shariffe's car. The walls are navy blue and the floor tiles are chequered blue and white.

"Vanessa," Shariffe whispers, breaking my concentration. "I'm so sorry for dragging you into this mess."

Before I can respond he scales the four steps in front of us and throws his hands into the air.

"I'm here to turn myself in!" he screams. "I have killed ten women and three men. My name is Shariffe, The Saw, Shakur and this is my beautiful wife and accomplice Vicious Vanessa Anderson," he points at me.

My heart drops from my chest and beats, like an unorganized marching band, in my stomach. I try to move but my feet are rooted to the ground.

"I love you so much Vanessa. You are the heartbeat that gave me the courage to stop the heartbeats of others," he says with a sinister grin before turning back to the room full of police officers. "My wife and I are here to face justice for our crimes. You will find body parts in a storage unit in Mississauga, and at my house inside of my freezer. My lovely wife has both of the keys in her pocket," he turns back to me. "Vanessa, my deadly darling, if you would be so kind as to hand me the two keys please."

My lungs cease breathing, the floor beneath me shifts suddenly, and I feel like I'm about to collapse. All of the officers sprint towards my stalker, swarming him like a heard of bees. I wait for them to throw him to the floor, force his hands behind his back and handcuff him before turning to me and demanding that I put my hands up but instead of detaining my stalker the officers are laughing and greeting him with hugs, smiles, fist bumps, and handshakes.

"When did you become a comedian?" A tall white officer with a clean-shaven face, golden blond head hair and broad muscular shoulders laughs while shaking Shariffe's hand.

"When are you going to become an actual cop?" Shariffe laughs.

"You always had a sense of humour, a bad one, but at least you had one. But then again, considering how you used to look, I'm sure you needed a sense of humour just to get up in the morning and look in the mirror. Remember how you looked when you first started growing out your hair?" he chuckles.

"How are you doing, Robert?" Shariffe grins.

"I'm doing fine, it's really good to see you again brother but what is going on with you why haven't you returned any of my phone calls?"

"I've been really busy as of late, forgive me brother."

"All is forgiven," Robert says while stepping in close to Shariffe. "But I really need a favour. Do you have anymore numbers and profiles?" Robert says, doing a horrible job a whispering.

"I don't do that anymore."

"I'm not asking you specifically to do anything, just give me your books and I'll do all the work, I'll even split the profit fifty-fifty with you."

"No."

"Sixty – forty."

"No."

"Shariffe you're killing me here but fine, seventy – thirty and that's the lowest I'm willing to go."

"I burnt everything last night, Robert."

"Tell me you're joking, Shariffe."

"I'm sorry, brother."

"What! Are you crazy? Why would you burn everything?"

"I had no choice, it was holding me back from getting what I truly wanted."

"You idiot," Robert whispers sharply, his face red with rage. "You always get caught up in some asinine trend with some asinine girl and then you lose your mind. You remember that time you almost got us indicted because you-"

"Robert," Shariffe cuts in. "This is my friend Vanessa and she is the only reason why I came here today. I did not come here to sell or give you anything. I need to have my police report printed so that she can take a look at it. So either get it printed or I'll go somewhere else and get it done."

Robert grimaces at Shariffe then looks over at me and smiles an obviously fake smile.

"So much for the brotherhood," he says before walking off.

Minutes later a female officer walks up to me and hands me a warm sheet of paper with Shariffe's name printed at the top of it.

I scan the report meticulously.

"So, am I a rapist?" He asks

"No."

"Am I a serial killer?" He chuckles.

"No."

"Then," he smiles. "Let's go home."

CHAPTER 11

TRAPPED

(Vanessa)

When you're depressed every place can feel like a prison
and every person can seem like a warden.

-

The Spirit of the Lord GOD is upon me, because the LORD has
anointed me to bring good news to the poor; he has sent me to
bind up the brokenhearted, to proclaim liberty to the captives,
and the opening of the prison to those who are bound;

Isaiah 61:1
****

In all of my life, I have never seen so much beauty so perfectly
organized in one location. Every direction I look I am
bombarded by an array of potent bright gardens filled to the
brim with lush flowers. Small furry forest animals run across
fields of dark green grass meanwhile families of birds flit from
large oak and pine trees. Shariffe's front yard is nothing like
the front yards in the city, nothing like the dehydrated lots with
a single malnourished tree barely protruding out from dead
ground. Shariffe's yard is alive, abundantly alive.

***

I throw the small, rusty, door open and exit the foul smelling
vehicle as quickly as I can. Happily, I inhale long overdue
breaths of fresh air before following behind Shariffe and
entering his mansion. The interior of his home is nothing like
the interior of his car; his home is lavish and unapologetically
expressive of wealth and privilege. Elegant window curtains
pout like thick strawberry red lips waiting for a lover's kiss,
large iridescent chandeliers hang elegantly from high ceilings
and there are flowers and plants everywhere.

"Who else lives here?" I ask.

"Nobody."

"You live here by yourself?"

"Yes."

I don't believe him.

"Who decorated your home?" I ask as my eyes survey the bounty of feminine beauty that surrounds me.

"I did," he smiles. "I decorated every room."

I can't imagine his big brutish frame desiring rose curtains or glass chandeliers, a woman must have requested all of these things.

"If you have all this money, why do you drive that old, rundown, car?"

"It forces me to be honest."

"Honest about what?"

"About who I really am, about the fact that all of this glitter and glamour that I've surrounded myself with really means nothing."

"Who are you, really?"

"Just a common, ordinary, man," he says with a rich boastful utterance that seems to contradict his words.

We leave the living room and enter a massive room filled with purple plants, dark purple walls and soft white carpets. The room smells of wet pine and is furnished with beautiful ivory coloured couches and large abstract paintings. Large paintings that according to Shariffe depict universal divide, the anarchy of man's nature, the collateral beauty in death and the unacknowledged horrors of birth but all I see are messy blobs of paint thrown recklessly unto three white canvases.

The next room that he shows me is by far the most beautiful room I have ever seen in my life. I inhale and a smile forms on my face as my nose fills with the sweet scent of the yellow roses that surround me.

This is how the other side lives!

This is what it means to be rich!

I love it.

I want it.

I need it.

I need it all!

I now understand why wealthy men and women are willing to do whatever they have to do to keep their money and

assets safe; money completely enhances the human experience, money makes life worth living. Money protects you from a multitude of heartaches and disappointments; money solves a majority of life's problems. "This is it," Shariffe beams with joy. "This is the Ital Factory, this is where I cook all of my masterpieces."
Before I can respond my right eye begins to twitch uncontrollably. Something large falls to the ground behind me and shatters into what sounds to be a million tiny pieces.
I turn in every direction, seeking out the source of the sound.
I can hear large, heavy, feet thudding all around me.
I continue searching, without luck, for the source of the sound.
My heart beats faster as the footsteps get louder and seem to transform from one loud unified thud into twelve separate but equally loud thuds. I continue to look around in a panic. I'm standing in the middle of a large open room with entrances all around me; whatever is coming for me could enter the kitchen and attack me from any direction. I search the room for something that I can use to defend myself. There is a large knife sitting in an iron rack by the kitchen sink. Before I can get to the knife three massive beasts storm into the kitchen. The beasts look me dead in my eyes and then roar loudly before charging towards me with their razor sharp mouths opening and closing as they approach.
I scream and grab hold of Shariffe's arm, pushing him in front of me as a sacrificial shield.
"*Atzor!*" Shariffe roars, his voice echoing in the large mansion and causing the creatures to stop dead in their tracks. "Vanessa," he says, his voice once again calm and soft as he turns to face me. "Please, forgive them they are still puppies and they get a little excited whenever they smell someone new, but they are harmless. They want to sniff you and lick you, that's all... do you mind?"
My eyes remain fixed on the devilish hounds. Their long black tongues are hanging from their mouths and they look hungry and far too large to be puppies.
"All three of you say sorry to Vanessa for scaring her."

The three creatures bark in unison, their loud howls shaking me to my core.

Shariffe laughs.

"See Vanessa? They are sorry. Now, would you like to pet them?"

I try to shake my head no but my neck along with my entire body refuses to move.

"Outside! Now!" Shariffe yells.

At his command the blood thirsty beasts scurry off.

"Now that they are gone," he says. "Allow me to show you to your room."

I try desperately to reject his offer and demand that he take me back to the hospital but it feels as if someone has glued my lips shut and stapled my tongue to the bottom of my mouth.

"Vanessa, are you ok?"

I force out a muffled cry for help.

"Vanessa, please forgive me but this is going to hurt," he says, pinching my right arm.

I jump from my stupor and scream out in pain.

"Welcome back," he smiles.

"I have to leave! I have to get out of here," I say in a panic.

"Leave? But you just got here."

"I don't care, I want to leave right now."

"You have nowhere to go though."

"It doesn't matter, take me back to the hospital."

"But-"

"Take me back to the hospital!" I scream.

"No," he says solemnly.

"What??"

"I'm sorry, but you can't leave."

"Can't?" I yell, my voice swelling with a mixture of rage and fear. "Who do you think you are? You don't own me; I can do whatever I want. You can't force me to stay here."

"You're right," he nods sombrely, his eyes void of feeling and his voice cold and heartless. "Technically, you *can* do whatsoever you want. But," his voice deepens and his eyes transform from empty circles to threatening rings of fire. "I am not going to let you leave. Now, Vanessa, would you like to see your room? I decorated it myself."

CHAPTER 12

WALLS

(Vanessa)

Often times we build fortified concepts and adhere to stringent philosophies in hopes of protecting ourselves from the abuses of others, but sometimes those same philosophies and concepts become walls that prevent us from experiencing the love of others.

"I will restore health unto thee, and I will heal thee of thy wounds, saith the LORD"

Jeremiah 30:17
****

I don't remember falling asleep but when I wakeup it is morning There are tears streaming from my eyes and my body is curled up in the foetal position. I want yesterday to be nothing more than a lucid nightmare, but the large, extra soft, king-sized mattress that I'm curled up on, along with the plush expensive sheets that cover my entire body, confirm my fears. The room I'm trapped in is elegant and spacious but the all white doors, all white carpet, and all white walls leave me feeling like I'm being caged in a small mental institution. Every single thing in the room is white, the sheets, the furniture, the clock, the curtains, the ceiling, the headboard, the footboard... everything.

'I decorated it myself,' I remember him saying.

He's trying to drive me crazy, he's messing with my mind. He's trying to break me down. He's mocking me, letting me know that he thinks I'm crazy for coming home with him.

I take a deep breath and do my best to remain calm; if I'm going to survive I have to remain calm. I continue to wander the white room with my eyes, searching for anything that I can use to my advantage like a nail clip with the little knife thingy or a small but sturdy decoration that I can use to hit him over the head with when he's not looking. I search and I search but there is nothing in the room that I can use as a weapon or to communicate with the outside world.

'I decorated it myself,' his cruel, menacing voice echoes in my head once again.

He must have been planning this from the first day he saw me at the grocery store.

But why me?

Why would anybody want to abduct somebody like me?

I'm not pretty.

I have no money.

I'm not -

The answer hits me like a heavy-handed punch to the nose, causing my eyes to water. He chose me because he has been following and observing me, he knows that I'm not anything to anyone, he knows that nobody loves me, which means that nobody will be looking for me. I'm the perfect victim, he can do whatever he wants to me, for as long as he desires, and no one will know or care that I am missing.

There is a knock on the room door.

I wipe my face clean and try to compose myself.

"Vanessa," his deep, coarse, voice charges through the white door and sits like an elephant on my chest. "Are you awake?"

I want to cry out but I purse my lips tightly, and remain as silent as possible. I need him to leave; I can't face him right now. I need time to compose myself and develop a plan.

The knocks get louder, violently shaking the large white door, "Vanessa, is everything ok in there? Are you alright?"

I don't answer.

There is a drawn out, disconcerting, period of silence.

I listen to hear if he is walking away.

"Vanessa? .... Vanessa," he roars. "Are you still in there? Vanessa... Vanessa!"

"Yes," I answer, my voice cracking under the weight of my situation.

"Do you mind if I come in?"

"Yes... I mean no.... I mean yes...."

"Yes I can come in or yes you mind?"

"Yes, you can come in," I sniffle.

The door opens.

He enters.

At the sight of him my chest compresses and my lungs tighten. He is taller and broader than I remember and in his massive right hand is a tiny cup of steaming hot tea. He grins menacingly at me and then stomps, troll-like, towards the bed. My heart is pounding out of control and I have no idea what to do. Every documentary that I've ever watched regarding being abducted claims that the abductee should strategically submit to his or her captor. If the abductee wants to stay alive the abductor must be made to feel at ease but more importantly the abductee must continue to be human in the eyes of the abductor. According to the documentaries I shouldn't beg or give up my agency but I also shouldn't challenge the authority of my abductor until the time is right.

"Do you mind if I sit down beside you, Vanessa?"

The correct answer, the answer that will pacify him and keep me safe for the moment is – *'no sir, of course I don't mind please sit down right beside me, oh and is that a cup of Ital tea? It smells amazing I'd love to try some,'* - but instead of responding in this way my mouth stays sealed and my eyes and facial features scream what my lips are too terrified to say.

He walks away from the bed and places the white cup of tea on the white nightstand next to the white clock.

I stare uneasily at the white cup; I won't let him break me so easily.

"I know that this whole situation is weird for you."

I nod my head.

"This is weird for me as well," he continues.

"Then don't do it."

"I can't not do it Vanessa, I have to listen to God."

"No you don't," I cry out. "You don't have to listen if you don't want to. Just let me go. I won't tell anyone what you did. Nobody has to know. I promise, I won't get you in trouble."

"Vanessa, you're not my prisoner."

My voice is shaky and low, "Then... then why can't I leave?"

"You *can* leave."

I rise slowly from the bed.

"I just cannot *let* you leave right now," he finishes.

I sink back into the white sheets, allowing them to imprison me once more.

I try to look him in his eyes in hopes of creating some kind of emotional connection but I can't stare at him without feeling uneasy in the pit of my stomach, so I turn away from him and say, "Then when? When can you let me leave?"

"I don't know Vanessa, that's up to God. I have to do what He says."

"Please, please!" I cry out. "I know that you believe that god is talking to you but believe me he isn't. It's just your thoughts. Your mind, your brain is tricking you. You have the wrong person. I don't even believe in god."

He turns his head away from me and gazes out the large room window.

"The sun is shining," he says randomly. "Would you like to go for a walk with me?"

"Please, Shaawreafe," I beg. "Please, please, just let me go. I... I... I won't tell anyone, I swear on my life."

"It's Shariffe," he smiles. "And I'm sorry Vanessa but nothing you say will change my mind. Now, would you like to go for a walk with me? I would really enjoy your company."

I exhale and turn away. I understand now that he is not the type of person who can be reasoned with or moved by tears and emotions. If I want to reclaim my freedom I will have to take more drastic actions.

"I'm, I'm very sorry, Mr. Shariffe, sir," I say while wiping my face clean of all liquids. "Yes, I would love to go for a walk with you, sir."

"You don't have to call me Mr. or sir or apologize to me, you haven't done anything wrong. Anyhow, I will leave you to get dressed. When I had your apartment cleaned out I asked the movers to write down all of your measurements including your shoe sizes. Everything in the closet should fit you perfectly. All the clothes, shoes, and jewellery are brand new. I'll wait for you downstairs."

When the white door clicks shut and I can no longer hear his large feet walking away I get up from my bed and walk to the closet. I slide open the large white door and gaze in disbelief. I have never been one for high fashion and fancy things but I can't help but be a little overjoyed at the small department store of colourful and elegant garments hanging before me. I enter the vast closet like a young child entering a candy store for the first time. I run my fingers across every piece of fabric, losing myself in their softness and their scent. I haven't inhaled the therapeutic scent of new clothes in forever. I love it and it's all mine! I own it all! *'What are you doing? You are a prisoner not a princess. He has abducted you not rescued you. Do not let him fool you with all of these pretty things. He is a controlling monster, he is trying to manipulate you, he is dangerous, you have to escape before he kills you,'* my inner self reminds me.

***

After walking for what feels like forever, the wide dirt path narrows and then comes to an abrupt end at a large red brick wall. I approach the wall and run the tips of my fingers back and forth across its rugged surface, discretely pressing hard against it in an attempt to check for any points of weakness.

"You must really love walls," he says with a chuckle.

I withdraw my hands and turn to face him, "No, actually, I hate walls. I prefer doors, open ones."

He laughs, "We have something in common then, I can't stand walls either. To be honest, they make me feel trapped, like a prisoner."

I shake my head and roll my eyes, "Then why is your entire house surrounded by one?"

"You'd have to ask the builders that question. With that being said though... If you hate walls so much why do you surround yourself with so many of them?"

"What are you talking about?"

"Who is Andrew?"

I grimace, "How... How do you know him?"

"I don't know him."

I stare at him, waiting for an explanation.

"You were screaming his name last night. The fact that you are physically here with me, but you are having nightmares about some person named Andrew means that you are afraid of me only because you are afraid of Andrew. You are allowing your experiences with Andrew to ruin your experiences with me, so the sooner you and I kill Andrew the sooner you and I can begin to bond."

My eyes grow wide with shock.

"So tell me," he continues. "Who is Andrew? Where does he live and would you like me to kill him by myself or would you like to do it together? What size gloves do you wear? We could even bury him right here," he stomps his right foot. "Nobody would ever find him, trust me," he grins. "How tall is he and how much do you think he weighs? I'll have to start digging the hole today if we want it ready in time for him. How does next week Tuesday sound to you?"

"What?" I exclaim. "I... I don't want to kill anyone."

He laughs, "I'm joking, Vanessa. Remember you said I look like a serial killer?"

He is crazier than I thought.

I need to get out of here.

I need to escape right now.

"Sorry, no more murder jokes, I promise. But who is Andrew and what did he do to you?"

Andrew's name echoes harshly in my ears, the memories of what he did to me flood me and I feel myself dying all over again. A large hole opens up in the pit of my stomach and I can feel it sucking me in. I feel sick and dizzy, everything around me is spinning and rising and falling quickly as if I am on an out of control rollercoaster. Without warning, my abductor charges like a raging bull towards me. I try to move out of the way but my entire body goes limp and everything around me goes black.

*

"Vanessa, this is your Uncle Andrew," my mother flickers, her face filled with the joy of a drowning woman who has been pulled aboard a sturdy ship. *"We will be living with him from now on because your father is a horrible man. Andrew is a*

*good man and he is helping us honey, so you have to be a
good girl and do whatever he tells you to do. Okay?"
I nod my head and smile.*

*Twenty-seven months, two weeks, and three days
later Andrew would transform from my uncle to my stepdad
and then from my stepdad to a dad who constantly stepped
across a forbidden line.*

*Standing at the foot of my bed, Andrew grabs hold of my
tiny body and tosses me high into the air but this time, unlike
all the times before, he doesn't catch me and cradle me
lovingly in his arms. This time, he stands indolently and
watches as my body comes crashing down onto my small
mattress.*

*"Throw me again, throw me again! I want wings, I want to
fly like a real angel," I beam.*

*I reach towards him but there would be no more flying, no
more rising and falling, now there would only be falling... a
deep never-ending fall.*

*Scratching, biting, crying and screaming out in pain I try to get
him to stop, I try to push his body off of mine but his body is
heavy and my little arms aren't strong enough to resist his
advances.*

*"Stop! Stop!" I yell. "Mommy help," I cry. "Jesus, mommy,
God," I cry but none of them come to save me.*

*"Vanessie, I want to play," my little sister Susan pushes my
bedroom door open and wobbles in. "Vanessie... Vanessie, I
want to play... Vanessie... Vanessie...*

*

"Vanessa... Vanessa... Vanessa."

When I regain consciousness and reopen my eyes my
abductor is there, he is cradling me in his arms and staring at
me.

"Put me down!" I yell, pushing and slapping until he is
forced to free me from his grip.

Tears are running down my cheeks, I can feel them
rushing like large rivers that have broken free from a weak
enclave. I wipe them away but they keep coming... I... I can't
cry in front of him... he'll... he'll think I'm weak... he'll use my

weakness against me... I'll be trapped here forever.

My captor steps towards me with his arms open.

I flinch and try to take a step back but the brick wall stops me.

"Don't touch me! Don't touch me," I cry out in vain as his large arms wrap around me, pulling me into his chest.

"Vanessa, we all have scars and your scars should not cause you hurt or shame. Your scars should remind you that whatever wounded you was not strong enough to kill you," he says softly.

Pushing myself free of him, I run down the expanding dirt path. My eyes are teary, and everything is a blurry haze as I move quickly past a cacophony of browns, greens, and greys. I'm wheezing, and sweating, I feel like I'm going to faint but I keep running.

I need to escape.

I need to be alone.

I need to get out of here.

I need to go home.

CHAPTER 13

TRIBULATIONS
(Vanessa)

God! If You truly exist, if you're not just a figment of my imagination or a fictitious character in a story book then I am begging you to help me, to save me... please.

-

"God is our refuge and strength, a very present help in trouble."

Psalm 46:1
****

I'm standing next to a young child. Together she and I stare out of a small window, watching as an old white car pulls out of the driveway. As soon as the white car drives out of sight, the little girl runs inside of her closet and quietly closes the door.

"You don't hide from monsters in a closet, that's where they live, that's where they get their power," I sigh.

The room door opens and Andrew enters, he heads straight for the closet shrouding his misdeeds in darkness but I know what happens next.

He'll ask the little girl, "Why are you hiding?"

The girl will sob and say, "Be... because you're going to hurt me and... and I don't want you to hurt me."

Andrew will say, "No my Angel, I would never ever hurt you. I love you."

Crouched fearfully in a small corner, with her back curved and her tear filled face buried deep into her knees, the child will say, "But... but I... I don't want to be your angel anymore. I... I want to stay a regular girl. I don't want wings, I don't want to go to heaven. I don't want you to love me."

"But don't you want to fly in the sky and be close to God?" he'll ask her.

"No," she'll answer. "I don't like God. I hate God. I wish God were dead."

Minutes later the closet door reopens and Andrew emerges alone.

"God, forgive me," he murmurs, while looking at the ceiling. "I am so sorry, God! I am sorry," he cries out. "I hate myself, why can't I stop these feelings? I don't deserve to live... Please God, kill me, kill me right now!"

"Vanessie, I want to play. I want to play!"

Andrew turns around, "Susan, what are you doing in here baby?"

"Play, play, play... where is Vanessie?"

"I think she is hiding. Do you want to help me find her? Do you want to be my little helper?"

"Yes, yes! Find Vanessie and play."

He scoops Susan up in his arms, twirls her around, kisses her on her forehead and then exits the room.

I walk to the closet and look inside. Crying in a corner is the little faceless girl. I want to hug the young girl, I want to kiss her on her cheeks, I want to wash and scrub her clean, I want to tell her that everything is going to be fine. I want to tell her that she will survive this, that she is not dirty, that it is not her fault, and that she should continue loving herself because she is worthy of love but I... I can't.

I close the closet door and lock it, trapping her inside and muffling her cries.

*

I'm awakened by the strange sounds of high-pitched giggling and loud discordant singing. When I sit up I notice that my room door has been pushed wide open and there is a little girl in a wrinkled green dress walking towards me.

I rub my eyes.

I must still be dreaming; it didn't occur often but once in awhile I would wake from one lucid nightmare only to find myself unknowingly trapped in another. I stare intently at the ghost child and concentrate all my mental power in an attempt to force her from my mind but no matter how hard I concentrate the child refuses to vanish.

"Shut up!" I scream, throwing the white covers off my body and flailing my hands in a dramatic display of power and bravery. "You're not real! You don't exist! Get out of here! Get out of my mind right now!"

"Ahhh... Monster! Mooonnnsssstteeer!" the little girl screams in a high-pitched squeal before turning quickly and fleeing from my room.

I sigh a sigh of relief then close my eyes and concentrate all my mental power on waking myself up. It takes some time but eventually all sound and sensation cease and I can feel the dream world that I'm trapped in slowly deconstructing around me. I feel myself re-entering reality when the sounds of loud heavy footsteps break my concentration.

I open my eyes.

Shariffe is standing at the entrance of my room, his large brutish frame enveloping my doorway. I expel all fear from my being and stare Shariffe right in his eyes.

"You're not real, leave me alone!" I scream boldly. "You can't keep me here. You don't control me! I am not afraid of you, I am not your prisoner. I am free! I am free!" I chant.

"Vanessa? Ummm, are you... Are you feeling alright?" the apparition asks.

"Shut up, you're not real!" I scream louder. "Get out of my mind, get out of my mind!"

"That's what she said to me too. I told you she was mean, and she uses really bad words."

My face contorts with shock as the small voice of a young girl emanates out from behind the imaginary image of Shariffe.

"Vanessa, I would like to formally introduce the lovely and esteemed Princess Candice," he says as he steps inside of my room and moves to one side, revealing the little girl in the wrinkled green dress.

I stare long and hard at the child and then look back at Shariffe.

"She came to me crying," he continues. "She said that you screamed at her and that you told her that she wasn't real...?"

I look at the little girl again, her face is flush with anger and her arms are folded at her chest. I don't know what to do or say, I'm not sure if I'm dreaming or not.

"She's pretty upset with you Vanessa, you may want to say sorry," laughs Shariffe.

"I'm sorry?" I say.

"And tell me that I'm real, and that I exit," she demands.

"Exist," Shariffe whispers, while struggling to hold back a smile.

"Yeah," she says boldly. "Tell me that I exissss... exissstss."

"You're real? You exist?" I say uneasily, not sure if I believe my own words.

"You see," he says, bending down so he is at eye level with the child. "I told you that she is a nice person... and guess what?"

"What?" The child beams, her eyes wide with anticipation.

"She is a princess, just like you."

"She's a princess... like me? Her?" Candice gasps, glancing at me in disbelief. "No she isn't."

"Of course she is," Shariffe says, animating his voice. "I mean just look at her, can't you tell a princess when you see one? Ohhh," Shariffe laughs. "I know why you can't see it."

"Why... Why can't I see it?"

"Because you aren't wearing your glasses."

Shariffe connects the index finger and thumb on both of his hands to form a circle; he then places the two circles around Candice's eyes.

"Ohhhh, ya..." Candice exclaims. "I see it, I see it now," she looks at me and giggles. "Is she your princess?"

"Of course not silly. Everybody knows that you can't own a princess, she's her own princess," he smiles, removing his fingers from around her eyes. "Just like you're your own princess. Nobody owns you, and nobody owns her. Now, run back downstairs and play. You can no longer come up here while Vanessa is sleeping. This is her room now and she requires privacy, okay?"

"Are... are you going to give her a ring, and marry her, and kiss her on the lips, and have baaaabies?" Candice snickers.

"Downstairs, Candice," Shariffe says sternly.

"Shariffe has a girlfriend, Shariffe has a girlfriend."

"Candice," Shariffe says, his voice deepening with purpose.

Candice stops speaking, looks at me, smiles a gigantic smile before waving goodbye, running out from my room and into the hallway and heading back downstairs.

"Children..." Shariffe says. "She's amazing isn't she?"

"Who is she?" I ask.

"Let's go find her and then you can ask her for yourself."

"Why don't you just tell me?"

"Because then you would only know my perception of her and what you need to know is her perception of herself. I can't tell you who somebody else is, that's crazy, Vanessa."

Oh, but listening to a voice in your head and keeping me hostage isn't crazy?

I fake smile, "Fine, let's go find her."

After brushing my teeth and washing my face, I follow Shariffe down a series of long winding stairs. When we arrive on the main floor there are children everywhere, they are running around in the backyard, eating snacks in the kitchen, jumping on the couches in the living room and petting and playing with Shariffe's dogs.

"What... What is this? What are all these kids doing here?" I panic.

"What kids?" he looks around, turning his head quickly from side to side.

I stare at him in confusion, "You, you don't see them? Maybe this is a dream," I mumble.

"They're not real," he laughs aloud. "They don't exist."

I stare at him in contempt, refusing to acknowledge his juvenile attempt to insult me.

"I'm sorry," he stops laughing. "A year or so ago I started a non-profit organization called S.O.I.L. Seeds Of Immense Light. I believe that children are filled with unimaginable potential but like seeds they can only become trees, and produce good fruit, if they are nurtured in a loving environment that gives them room and freedom to grow. Every weekend I allow children from various foster homes and marginalized communities across Toronto to come to my mansion as an inspirational retreat."

"Why though? Why are you doing this?"

"I suppose I just want to make sure that they are happy and that they have a fair chance at life. I feel like I owe that to Candice, to all the children."

"Why though? Why do you owe it to them?"

"I just do, Vanessa."

"You just do?"

"Yes, Vanessa, I just do."

"Why? I want to know why," I say sternly.

"I'll answer later, I promise," he says quickly. "I just saw Candice running around outside. Let's go catch her before she disappears again."

"No."

"Why not? I thought you wanted to ask her who she is?"

"I don't care who she is anymore..." *I care who you are and the real reason why you have all these young, vulnerable, children running around your house.*

"Are you sure?" he asks.

"Yes, I'm sure."

"Okay... well... I'm going to try and catch her but I could still really use your help down here with the rest of these kids, if you don't mind."

"I'm going back to sleep, I'm already your prisoner, I'm not going to be your slave as well."

"You're not my prisoner, Vanessa."

When I arrive in my room I close the door behind me and walk quickly to the large open window and look outside. I search eagerly through the scattered crowd of children for a single adult who can help me to escape but the only adult I see is Shariffe. He has found Candice and they are sitting together under the shade of a tall Oak tree.

Shariffe glances up at my room window and our eyes meet. He smiles at me and waves but I can't help but feel disturbed. I feel it in the depths of my bones; there is something horribly wrong about him and I need to discover what but more than anything I need to protect Candice.

CHAPTER 14

LOCATION

(Vanessa)

You will never get to where you need to be and you will never become the person who you are destined to be if you stay where you know you're not meant to be.

-

I will lead the blind in a way that they do not know, in paths that they have not known I will guide them. I will turn the darkness before them into light, the rough places into level ground. These are the things I do, and I do not forsake them.

Isaiah 42:16
****

On the ninth morning of my captivity, I am forcibly awakened by a series of loud knocks on my room door.

"Vanessa!" My captor bellows, his savage voice rushing through the white door and brutally attacking my ears.

I grunt, grab hold of a large pillow and smother myself with it in an attempt to drown out his annoying voice.

"Vanessa! Are you awake?"

I ignore him but he continues to pound on my door with his hulky knuckles.

"Yes! Yes, I'm awake," I half scream. "What is it? What do you want?"

"Hurry up and get dressed, I need to show you something."

I glance at the white clock on my nightstand. Big red, digital, letters flash the numbers 4:58.

I groan and sigh in agony.

I want to scream, I want to cuss at him and call him every inappropriate word in the English language, I want to hit him over the head with the white clock and knock him unconscious but more than anything in the world I just want to go back to sleep!

"Vanessa, are you coming? You have to hurry up or we are going to miss it," his unrelenting voice comes again. "I'm coming," I grunt. "Can you just give me sometime ...ten more minutes, please?"

He sighs, "Ok, ok, but please you have to hurry up or we will miss it."

Fourteen minutes later I unwillingly rise from my warm, soft, bed and do as my captor commands. When I open my room door he is resting casually against the hallway wall. Today, he is wearing fitted sweatpants along with a plain white tee shirt and his long dreads are tied in a neat ponytail and he smells of cocoa butter and coconut oil.

'A man should always smell good, if a man smells bad it means he is unfit to be a husband and a father. A man who smells bad can't take care of a wife and kids.'

Shut up mom, it is far too early for your nonsense. Get out of my head before I come in there and throw you out myself.

My mother complies, exiting my mind without fight.

I follow Shariffe up a short flight of espresso coloured wooden stairs that take us to a long beautiful hallway that leads into a small dimly lit room. The room is empty except for a small orange coffee table, a vase full of small sunflowers and a long yellow sofa that faces a large window.

"What did you want to show me?"

"Make yourself comfortable, Vanessa. We still have a few minutes before it arrives," he says, gesturing me to the couch that he is already sitting on.

"I'm fine, I'll stand."

"Please, I insist."

I sigh within myself and like the obedient prisoner that I am I do as I am commanded. He has chosen to strategically sit on the middle cushion of the couch, which means that no matter where I sit I will be sitting uncomfortably close to him.

"Would you like a Kale and Spinach Smoothie?"

"No."

"Ital Juice?"

"No."

"Almond Milk?"

"No."

"Alkalized Coconut Water or Plain Water?"

"The only thing I want is to know why you woke me up at five in the morning and dragged me to this small room."

He smiles, "This small room is one of the main reasons why I bought this big house."

I look around the barren room a second time, "What's so special about it?"

"It's location. Location influences every single aspect of our existence. Location dictates what we see and what we do not see, what we hear and what we do not hear, what we feel and what we do not feel, which in turn determines what and how we think. The thoughts that we think then dictate the actions that we take and the actions that we take determine the life that we live. Everything starts with our location," he raises his hands in the air as if his words are deep and philosophical as if I'm supposed to be impressed by his mindless babbling. "This room is the perfect location, it-."

"Can you please just hurry up and show me this thing so that I can go back to bed?" I interrupt.

"Patience Vanessa, patience is also very important. This thing cannot be rushed, I can't force it to come before its time."

I exhale and allow my eyes to wander the cramped yellow room while I wait for something spectacular and otherworldly to happen.

Ten long excruciating minutes pass... nothing happens.

Another ten minutes pass and still nothing, this great thing that he speaks of, this thing that demands patience and the perfect location has yet to arrive.

"Life on earth as we know it could not exist without the sun," he says suddenly, his voice low and stoic as if in a trance. "The sun forces us to acknowledge that our lives and our ability to appreciate and perceive ourselves and others is dependent on the existence of a more prevalent and powerful force. The sun is so beautiful, it humbles us and yet at the same time it exalts and glorifies us," he points toward the naked window.

In the horizon, the sky is slowly being set on fire by a surreal sea of oranges, yellows, pinks and bright reds.

"My mother loved watching the sunrise when she was alive," he continues, his eyes closed and his fingers extending and contracting slowly. "She used to tell me that the sun was created by God to give light and to enlighten by providing humans with a daily example of the way in which God loves us. The sun gives light, energy, and life to everything on the earth. And just like the sun, depending on our location we may be unable to see and feel God but just like the sun, God is always there. He never leaves us no matter what we do or say. Sometimes, we just need to change our location in order to experience His warmth and light."

You woke me up to watch the sunrise! I'm infuriated but I holdback my anger and keep my lips pursed.

"Where are you?" he says, opening his eyes and turning his head so that he is now staring directly at me. "Right now Vanessa, where are you?"

"I'm sitting beside you, imprisoned in your house."

"Your body is here with me but your body is only a small portion of your existence. Where is the rest of you, where is your consciousness, where is your spirit? Where are you?"

"I don't know what you're talking about."

"Yes, you do," he says, his eyes now emitting a strange and intense glow. "Where are you? Who or what is holding you hostage?"

"I said, I don't know what you're talking about."

"We all have problems, Vanessa," he continues. "And sometimes God places people in our life that He can use to help us eliminate our problems. You can tell me what happened; whatever Andrew did or didn't do doesn't define you."

I grimace at him and grit my teeth, "So you believe god is the sun, you believe god provides light and warmth and all the good things and people who help us?"

"Yes," he says, nodding his head decisively.

"What about the people and things who hurt us? Who provides them? Who provides the cold, who provides darkness and death and pain?"

He stares deep into my eyes trying to use his creepy eye-ology thing to read me but I close my eyes and turn away.

"Tell me about Andrew," he says. "You were screaming his name again last night. Talk to me, Vanessa."

"Answer my questions," I demand.

"Vanessa," he says my name softly as if pitying me. "Whatever happened to you, whatever pain you went through, whatever sorrow you're experiencing God can and will use it for a higher purpose." "For a higher purpose," I scoff. "What makes your god's purpose for my life so much higher than my own purpose for my life? If your god wants me to suffer and cry every night but I want to be happy, why should I suffer just because your god has some higher purpose for my pain?" "Vanessa, who is Andrew? What did he do to you?" "None of your business, that's who Andrew is," I yell.

I wait for him to respond but he just sits there on his ugly yellow couch and stares at me with his ugly brown eyes and ridiculous looking dreadlocks.

"Oh, and by the way," I continue. "The sun in reality is nothing more than an unstable ball of nuclear energy that will eventually explode and kill us all. The sun causes cancer and forest fires and droughts and heatstroke, so if the sun represents your god's love then I'd prefer to stay far away from your god and his love."

He sits there, once again not moving or responding, he just sits there like a big black stupid mannequin.

"Can you hear me?!" I yell.

"I can hear you, Vanessa. I can hear you. Keep talking, I'm listening."

Grunting out of frustration I stand to my feet and storm out of the tiny room. As I walk down the dimly lit hallway towards the staircase my right eye begins to twitch and then suddenly I hear the floor creak loudly behind me. When I glance over my shoulder I see Shariffe charging towards me. I scream out and make a mad dash for the staircase but I stumble and fall hard and fast to the ground.

"Please..." I beg, throwing my hands up in defence. "Please... don't kill me. I'm sorry, I'm sorry, I'll do whatever you want, I'll-"

Before I can finish my sentence Shariffe speed walks around my balled up frame and disappears down the long set of stairs.

CHAPTER 15

SHARIFFE

****

Shariffe opens his eyes, stands slowly from his bed, spreads his arms wide and looks to the heavens. For the next ten minutes he refrains from moving and speaking, in his mind he devotes himself to praising and honouring his Creator, in his mind he thanks God for life, in his mind he thanks God for Vanessa, for Candice and all of the other blessings in his life. Upon completion of his morning devotion he performs his morning routine of high intensity stretches and body weight exercises. Once his routine is complete Shariffe enters his washroom where he brushes his teeth, washes his face and moisturizes his hair one lock at a time. The circular mirror that he stares into is cracked in the center and missing small pieces of glass but he refuses to have the mirror replaced. The accosted mirror, the wooden bracelet on his wrist, the scar on his right hand, the gold ring on his finger, and the photograph hanging on his room wall are all reminders of the man he used to be and what he went through to become the man he currently is. And, although he by no measure considers himself to be a good man, he does see himself as better than what he once was and for that he is proud.

Using a waterproof cloth, Shariffe wraps his hair before entering his standing shower and scrubbing his body. Emerging from the shower Shariffe picks up a small plastic bottle filled to the brim with beeswax, ginseng, olive oil, and ground up aconitum leaves and lathers his entire body. As the concoction soaks into his skin, a cool soothing sensation moves slowly throughout his body, relaxing his muscles and causing him to exhale.

On the wall next to the broken mirror is a picture that Candice has drawn; it is a drawing of a beautiful woman in a white dress. With tears in his eyes Shariffe turns away from the drawing, exits his washroom and sits on his king sized bed.

Rubbing his fingers through his rich black beard, he stares out his room window and imagines his, Vanessa's, and Candice's future life together. They would make the perfect family, he thinks to himself. He would be an amazing husband and an amazing father, he would love Vanessa the way a man should love his wife and he would love Candice the way a father should love his daughter. He would give them everything, his heart would live to serve and love them but the decision is not his to make.

"Help me, God," Shariffe asks. "I want to tell her everything but if I tell her the truth she'll think I'm a monster. How do I get her to trust me?"

Shariffe sits in complete silence, waiting for God to respond. Two hours later a bright red bird perches on his windowsill holding a large worm in its beak, seconds later a smaller brownish bird lands beside it. Shariffe watches intently as the larger bird breaks the worm into tiny pieces and patiently feeds and tends to the smaller bird.

CHAPTER 16

GARDEN
(Vanessa)

The love that you plant in someone else's heart will grow the tree that bares the fruit that in return makes your life sweet.
-
"Whoever brings blessings will be enriched, and one who waters will himself be watered."

Genesis 2:15
****

This morning I am not forced awake by a barrage of heavy handed attacks against my room door; instead, I wake to the sweet sound of a bright red cardinal singing his heart out to a smaller reddish brown female cardinal. In the horizon, behind the love-struck birds, rays of bright sunlight penetrate the dusk sky and cause it to bleed lush streams of pink and red. As I watch the sky bleed I can't help but remember back to red blood, warm like sunshine, streaming out from inside of me and rolling down my young black thighs.

Suddenly, my room door flies open and like a mad man Shariffe comes charging in causing the two birds to fly away.

"What the heck are you doing?!" I scream, pulling my bed sheets up to my neck.

"I'm sorry, I'm so sorry, please forgive me. It'll never happen again and I didn't see anything I swear but Vanessa we have to get started," he says in a rush while placing down a large tray of food and a glass of one of his dark green vegetable juices on my nightstand. "You're going to need a lot of energy today, Vanessa. We have a lot of work to do."

"What are you talking about? Get started on what?"

"Gardening," he says. "We have to garden."

"Gardening? I don't want to garden."

"But, I can't do it without you. I need your help Vanessa and the sooner we finish gardening the sooner I can let you leave... I think."

"You think?"

"Yes, I think," he pauses. "The truth is I'm just as much in the dark as you are about this whole thing that we are experiencing together but I trust God and I know for certain that He wants you and I to Garden. I think it'll bring us closer together."

"I don't want us to be closer together."

"Oh, ummm... please?" he smiles.

I shake my head and sigh. This is only the beginning of his proposition and I am already tired of hearing him talk and I know that if I say no he will be in my room all day trying to convince me to say yes. That is the thing about crazy people, they are firm in their convictions, they cannot be swayed by reason or truth or money the only way to stop a crazy person is to kill them.

***

When Shariffe and I arrive at the garden, he drops the large bag of seeds that he was carrying on his shoulders unto the ground and then immediately falls to his knees and begins to work. Apprehensively, I drop to my knees and follow his lead. Together he and I work in his garden, digging small holes, planting seeds and uprooting weeds. This is my first time gardening and it is harder than I could have ever imagined, I'm sweating and panting, my back hurts from bending and my neck is sore. My hands are cold and my clothes are muddy and wet. Insects won't stop buzzing around my ears and I can't use my fingers to scratch my nose or massage my neck or back because my hands are covered in dirt.

I hate gardening!

When I look over at Shariffe he is smiling, he is like a gigantic pig playing in a mountain of mud. Even the large pile of dirt alongside him seems to be moving and dancing happily.

I lean forward, focus my gaze on the pile and look closer. I scream aloud and back away quickly.

"What's wrong? Are you ok?" He asks, dropping his hoe and turning towards me. "Did something bite you?" "Beside you," I point. "The dirt... the dirt is moving." He looks down, "This?" He laughs. "They're just worms. If you find any please toss them in the pile with the others." "I'm not touching any worms." "Your loss," he says. "They make great snacks, especially if they are pregnant with a crispy batch of eggs in their clitellum."

Shariffe picks up a large brown worm from the moving pile and brings it inches from his face and then opens his mouth wide and sticks out his tongue. The creature curls and twirls in his hand. A sharp chill shoots through my body causing me to squirm and turn away.

"Wait a minute, I can't eat this worm. It's all covered in dirt."

I open my eyes just in time to see Shariffe drop the creature back into the moving pile of other worms.

"I'm joking, Vanessa. We're going to need these worms for the indoor plants, they help the plants grow."

I shake my head and return to gardening. He is by far the strangest man I have ever met. Everything he does is a contradiction yet every contradiction that he commits somehow allows him to live in what seems to be perfect harmony. Imprisoning me to provide me freedom? He is always cleaning, the inside of his house is spotless and pristine, but when he is outside he is the dirtiest person in the world. Nothing about him makes any sense. But I know that people like him, people who are double minded yet at peace are the craziest, and most dangerous of all. So despite how nice and harmless he may seem I will never let my guard down.

Two hours later, the pile of worms has doubled, all the weeds have been uprooted and the large bag of seeds that I feared would never finish is finally empty. I stand to my feet, ready to head back inside, but Shariffe remains kneeling beside his worms. He closes his eyes and then inhales deeply before picking up a handful of dirt, smelling it and then rubbing it intimately between his fingers.

This is the perfect opportunity.

There is a large jagged stone by my foot that I unearthed secretly while he and I was gardening.

I will only have one shot at this.

I close my eyes and imagine every move before I make it. I see myself bending down, picking up the large stone and then smashing it repeatedly into the back of Shariffe's head. No, not the back of his head, his dreads will act as a helmet and stop the stone in its tracks. I will have to hit him on the front of his head, just above his eyes. While he is knocked out I'll run inside, grab the key to one of his Jeeps and then crash my way through the front gate and drive to freedom.

I bend down and pickup the stone.

On the count of three, he's going to get a face full of stone.

I take a deep breath and position myself perfectly.

1... 2... 2 and a half... 2 and three quarters...

Shariffe stands to his feet a quarter of a second before I am ready to unleash my wrath on him. I sigh, drop the stone from my hand and use my left foot to recover it with dirt.

"I used to wonder," he says. "Why God chose to place Adam and Eve in a garden when He could have placed them anywhere He wanted and then one day the answer came to me. God was sending all of humanity a message. He was letting us know that we are His flowers and He is our sun and if we hope to grow and blossom then we must reach for Him the way flowers reach for the sun. It is so simple, reach for goodness, reach for the thing that by it's design stimulates your growth and you are bound to grow."

"God's flowers?" I scoff under my breath.

I know the story of Adam and Eve very well: In a perfect garden, created by a perfect God, there existed a deadly forbidden tree, an evil serpent, an unhappy man, and a poor naïve woman. The fact that a God who can do no wrong was able to create such disharmony, depression, and ignorance never made sense to me. Even as a child, the idea of a perfect being creating imperfection was ludicrous to me. The Adam and Eve story proved either that God is imperfect or what we consider imperfection is actually perfection to God.

"Do you know what we just planted?" he asks.

"No."

"Aconitum napellus. It's poisonous."

I stare at him suspiciously, "Why were we planting poison?"

"To poison people... why else would we plant poison? Do you have anyone that you would like to poison?"

Yes, you! Can we poison you?

I keep my thoughts hidden away and stare at him blankly. He smiles at me, waiting for me to respond to his outlandish statement. As I stare at his stupid face all I keep thinking is I really, really, wish I had hit him in his face with that stone.

"In Ancient Rome," he continues. "Aconitum was used by conquered emperors and warriors to commit a painless suicide when a horrible death at the hands of their enemies seemed inevitable, but in Ancient Egypt aconitum was used as a medicinal ointment on princes and pharaohs in order to soothe their sore muscles," he says before inhaling a large gulp of air and taking off his rubber boots.

I cringe in disgust as I watch him playing in the dirt with his toes. He is so filthy, I think to myself as the sound of wet dirt slopping beneath his feet rises to my ears.

"Vanessa, I think Jesus is showing you and I that nothing in this world is absolutely evil or poisonous. People can and will plant seeds in our lives, but the choice is ours whether or not we are going to allow those seeds to poison us or heal us. Is God saying anything to you, Vanessa? Do you hear or feel anything?"

"Yes," I say while still staring at his oversized bootless feet.

"What is He saying to you?" he asks excitedly.

"God says that you should let me go."

He laughs, "I know, He told me that as well, but the time hasn't come yet."

I sigh and roll my eyes.

"Vanessa, you don't want to be here with me, I get that. But seeing as you are here with me, and you're not leaving, why not just make the best out of it? If you try hard enough you can find the good in anything, try to find the good in me and our situation... please."

I exhale, roll my eyes and fold my arms.

"Please," he says again.

"What about the snake?" I say. "Your god created and allowed the snake to live in the garden and according to Christians the snake is pure evil."

"The spirit that entered the snake was and is pure Evil but through that evil spirit God was able to provide a perfect example of His unconditional love. God was able to show all of humanity that His love has the power to get rid of our mistakes, but our mistakes do not have the power to get rid of His love."

"So let me get this straight, your God created a forbidden tree that could kill humans, and an evil talking snake that would basically tempt humans to commit suicide and then He put these three opposing entities in one location to basically battle it out with each other, yet you still believe that your God loves and wants the best for humanity?"

"Yes."

"That makes no sense."

"There can be no freedom, no happiness, no peace without choice and without knowledge of that choice. A castle without a door in which to exit is nothing more than a pretty dungeon. If you are forced to live somewhere you will never be able to grasp the infinite joys which that place holds because your mind will only focus on your inability to come and go as you feel. The tree and the snake were the necessary doors that transformed The Garden of Eden from a pretty prison to a wonderful paradise."

I want to ask him where my door out of this pretty prison is located, but before I am able to open my mouth and ask my question he continues speaking.

"Vanessa," he stops stomping in the mud and stares intently into my eyes. "These last twenty days with you have been some of the best days of my life, and I want to say thank you," he smiles at me as he unknots the garden hose and uses the now free flowing water to wash his muddy feet.

As I watch him wash the dirt from his feet his kind words wash over me and as sad as it may sound, I share his sentiment. I am happy that he abducted me. When I was free I was lonely and sad, when I was free I desired death but since being abducted and forced to live in Shariffe's presence, I haven't thought about suicide once. For the last twenty days my mind has only been focused on preserving and enriching my life.

I know that these pathetic thoughts belong to my weak mother but I don't fight them. I submit to my mother, I let her win because at this moment her deplorable, archaic, way of thinking makes me happy.

***

By the time Shariffe and I finish speaking it is lunchtime. He picks up his pile of worms, drops them into two large metal buckets and then he and I head inside just minutes before rain begins to pour from the sky. Standing at the back entrance of the mansion Shariffe whistles three times, causing all three dogs to come rushing to the sliding door. The three beasts are soaking wet but they don't seem to want to stay inside where it is dry and warm. Reaching into the front pocket of his green overalls Shariffe hands me three bone shaped treats.

The animals turn and face me.

"Don't be afraid, you're in charge Vanessa, tell them what you want them to do and they will do it."

Apprehensively I say, "Sit."

They sit.

"La... la   lay down."

They lay down

"Play dead," I laugh without thinking.

They fall to the ground, close their eyes, and let their long black tongues hang from the side of their mouths.

"Stand up," I say confidently.

They stand to their feet, raising their heads in anticipation of their reward.

I smile, pet them, and then feed each one of them individually. My heart skips a beat every time one of their wet, rubbery, tongues make contact with my hand.

'What are you doing?' I hear my inner self ask. *'What if they bite you? Look how big they are, look how sharp their teeth are. Aren't you afraid? You should be afraid!!'*

When they finish eating Shariffe whistles, causing them to turn to him at which point he grabs each of them by their necks and pets them aggressively, pulling back the skin on their necks and shaking their heads before sending them back into the wetness of the yard.

For some strange reason I can't pull my gaze away from him, there is something so different about him, something special and unique that I desire to uncover. His tacky dark green overalls and black rubber boots fit his character and personality better than any high-end three-piece suit, fitted dress shirt and dress shoes ever could.

He looks so at peace, so majestic and strong.

I can't believe I ever thought about beating him to death with a stone.

"Vanessa," he says, jeering me back to reality. "Do you mind helping me drop these worms in the plants? I'll take upstairs and you can take downstairs."

"No," I say quickly. "I don't like worms they look like-" I bite my tongue and gasp.

"Look like what?" he asks.

"Snakes," I lie. "They look like snakes."

He stares deep into his bucket and then nods his head and shrugs his shoulders before saying, "Yeah... I... I guess they do kind of look like snakes. Ok," he smiles. "I'll be back and when I'm done we can get lunch started."

Shariffe and I part ways, he enters the living room and I enter the kitchen. As I sit and wait for him to finish sprinkling worms around the house, I think about how all the strange things that he does for me feels normal and right.

'Now just lose some weight, fix your hair, exfoliate your skin, wax your body hair, whiten your teeth and then maybe he will marry you and you can finally have some babies. You're getting old, you need a man and you need a baby, a woman is nothing without a man and a baby,' I hear my mother say.

I look down and grab hold of my large protruding stomach; I stretch the waist of my sweatpants and stare at my hairy legs in disgust.

"Maybe my mother is right, maybe I do need to lose some weight and start waxing."

Suddenly, my left eye twitches and the loud metallic ring of something large and heavy crashing to the ground fills my ears. Springing to my feet I sprint towards the source of the sound without thinking. When I arrive at the entrance of the living room I see Shariffe, he is slouched on the floor and there are worms and dirt scattered all around him.

I run towards him, gracefully avoiding the brown creatures wiggling on the floor.

"Shariffe," his name rolls off my tongue. "Are you ok? What happened? Are you hurt?"

"I'm fine," he smiles. "I just tripped."

I look around the room, scanning the floor for any protruding objects, "Over what?"

"My big feet," he laughs.

"How do you trip over your own feet?" I laugh back.

"So this is funny to you?"

"Yes," I laugh. "Very funny."

"Well then catch," Shariffe says before swiftly running his hands across the ground and scooping up a large pile of moving dirt and throwing his hand in my direction.

I close my eyes and scream aloud.

"Vanessa," I hear Shariffe laugh hysterically.

I open my eyes; Shariffe is sitting on the floor smiling at me his hand still full of the moving pile of dirt. I'm about to yell at him and tell him how childish and immature and disgusting he is being when I notice that his left arm is shaking.

"Your arm-"

"What's wrong?" He interrupts, brushing off clumps of dirt from his body. "Is it a worm? Did I squish it?"

"No... your left arm is shaking, are you sure you're ok?"

He looks down at his arm and laughs, "I guess I'm getting old, I shouldn't have worked out right before gardening."

"Shariffe."

"I'm fine, Vanessa."

CHAPTER 17

BELIEF
(Vanessa)

Children teach us the things that we try to teach them to forget,
like how to believe in something we cannot see and how to
believe that we are much more than what we do see.

-

"Children are a heritage from the LORD: and the fruit of the
womb is his reward. As arrows are in the hand of a mighty
man; so are children."

Psalms 127:3-4
****

I can feel her big brown eyes watching me, analysing me,
trying desperately to understand me so that she can label me
and place me in a nice simple box that can fit easily in her nice
simple world.

"Are you... umm... Are you really his princess?" she
giggles. "Because you don't dress like you're his princess."

Ignoring her, I continue washing and chopping fruits and
vegetables to put out for the other less invasive and
troublesome children to eat.

"He says you're a princess, but I don't believe him. If
you're a princess then why don't you have on a crown like I
do?"

I stop chopping, place the knife on the wooden cutting
board, and stare at Candice long and hard.

"And... and where is your dress?" She twirls around
allowing the bottom of her frilly gown to rise high into the air.
"If... if... if you're a princess," she says dizzily, almost toppling
over. "You should have on a dress and a crown like me.
Princesses don't dress like you, they dress like me. Look at
me, look at me, look at me, I'm a princess... you're not."

I shake my head and bite down on my bottom lip, doing
my best to keep my thoughts locked away in my head.

"Why aren't you wearing a princess dress, huh? Why aren't you wearing a princess dress like me? Huh? Huh? Tell me... tell me. Where is your crown? Huh, huh, huh, huh, tell me, huh, hu-"

"I'm not wearing a crown or a princess dress because I am not a princess and neither are you!" I declare sharply.

"If you're not a princess," she says smugly, both her hands on her hips, while staring me down. "Then why do you live in a castle with a prince?"

I shake my head and sigh out of frustration, "This isn't a castle Candice, this is just a really big house, and Shariffe isn't a prince he's just a regular man who has a lot of money. There are millions of men like him. Castles, princes, and princesses don't exist in the way you think they do."

"I don't believe you, you're wrong," Candice pouts, a steely expression clouding her owl eyes. "Shariffe is a prince and I am a princess and this is a castle. You said before that I didn't exist but look I do!" She declares, grabbing hold of the skin on her left arm and tugging on it. "Here, pull it, touch me... I'm real. See, see?" She offers me her arm as proof.

"This is different, Candice."

"No it isn't."

"Yes it is," my voice rises and becomes firm.

"No! No! No, it isn't!" She screams.

"Good day Princess Candice and Princess Vanessa."

When I look behind me Shariffe is on his knees, his massive, muscular, body rising and falling in reverence.

"You don't have to bow you're a prince," Candice giggles hysterically.

"I am? Ohhhh yeaaah, you're right, I am, I am. Sometimes I forget, it is a good thing that I have such a smart princess like you around to remind me," he says with a goofy smile on his face before standing to his feet.

"See!! I told you, I told you I am a princess! I was right and you were wrong," she boasts.

"No you're not!" I roar. "You're not a princess Candice! You're just a regular little girl!"

"No I'm not! I'm not just a regular little girl. You're wrong. I am a princess! You're regular! And, and, and you're mean!" She fights back with a winey yell. "I don't like you. I hate you. I hope Shariffe doesn't choose you to be his princess because you're mean and ugly and stupid!"

"Candice," Shariffe breaks in, his voice calm but stern.

Candice stops speaking immediately, her face wrinkles as if struggling to hold back tears.

"Ye... ye... yes," she sniffles. "Sha... Sha... Shariffe."

"What did I tell you about yelling at people and calling them bad names, especially adults?"

"That it isn't nice," she cries.

"Now, please say sorry to Princess Vanessa and then I would like for you to stop crying and go outside and play with the other children while Princess Vanessa and I have a talk."

Candice apologizes unwillingly then turns and runs out from the kitchen, her tiara falling from her head in the process. A part of me is sad that she is mad at me and that she thinks I'm mean, a part of me wants to impress her and wants her to like me and look up to me but more than anything I want to keep her safe and that can only be done by telling her the truth.

"Why are you lying to her?" I confront Shariffe.

"I'm not lying to her."

"Yes you are. She's not a princess."

"Prove it."

"What?"

"I want you to prove to me that she is not a princess. Where are your facts, where is your proof? Show me your research, I'll wait."

"Are you serious?" I roll my eyes and scoff.

"Yes, I'm dead serious," he answers, his eyes fixed on my face in a straight unwavering gaze. "You know very little about Candice, if anything at all, yet you claim that she isn't a princess even though she has told you repeatedly that she is. I'm sure if she told you that she was not a princess you would be quick to believe her, so why can't you be just as quick to believe her when she says that she is a princess? Why do you need her to be regular? Why can't she be special? And even if she isn't special to you why can't she be special to herself and to me, why do you need to break her? Just because you refuse to acknowledge her royalty doesn't mean she should give up her crown. So, if you don't have anything positive and constructive to say to Princess Candice," he declares firmly. "Then I kindly ask that you no longer say anything to her at all." This is the first time that Shariffe has ever been so stern with me. He isn't angry or shouting or threatening me but I can see it in his eyes and hear it in his voice that he is very serious, and that he will do whatever is necessary to make Candice happy and protect her.

Breaking eye contact, I shake my head and fold my arms in contempt, "Tell her the truth or I will. I won't let you lie to her."

"What is the truth Vanessa?"

"That this isn't a castle!" I can't stop myself from yelling or stop my body from trembling. "That you're not a prince and she's not a princess, that she doesn't live in a Disney movie, that fairy tales don't exist. Just... just stop it, just please stop lying to me Andrew-" I stop speaking abruptly. All the anger fades from my face and I am left only with the raw feeling of nakedness.

"Vanessa," Shariffe places his hand on my shoulder. "The truth is that Candice is a young child with her whole life ahead of her. What you say to her and the way you treat her will either build her or destroy her. I never told Candice that she was a princess. She came to me and declared that she was a princess; I just agreed and supported her. She is building her own world and I'm just providing the material and the encouragement until she can provide them for herself. Didn't you used to believe that you were something more than a regular child when you were younger?"

"No," I say flatly, trying to shake the lingering sensation of his touch.

"I used to pretend that I was a superhero. I wore my long johns as tights and I would wear my underwear over my long johns, I didn't care if my underwear was clean or dirty. Needless to say, nobody ever allowed me to rescue them, people ran from me like I was the villain," he laughs. "I bet you used to pretend you were a princess just like Candice. I can see royalty all over you."

I don't respond.

"A super hero? A knight? A doctor? A teacher? A... umm-"

"I used to have wings," I break in. "Like an idiot I used to believe that I was an angel, I used to believe that I could actually fly," my voice cracks, making it hard for me to speak. "Now all I have are these ugly scars that will never go away. I want you to tell her the truth Shariffe or I will. I'm not trying to hurt her or destroy her dreams. I just her to be safe, I don't want her to grow up and be like me, I don't want her to-" I stop speaking.

Shariffe draws me in and hugs me. I don't resist his embrace, I have grown to enjoy and yearn for the warmth of his hugs. Resting my head on his large chest I lose myself in the moment.

"Candice used to have a lot of scars as well, but she chose to replace those scars with a crown. Don't you think she deserves her crown, just as much as you deserve your wings?"

He releases me from his loving hold and then bends down, picks up Candice's crown and hands it to me.

"What am I supposed to do with this?"

"Whatever you choose to do with it," he says before walking out of the kitchen.

I lift the little plastic crown up to my eyes. The paint is striping from it, two of the three plastic diamonds are missing and the one that remains is dusty and old with a chip in the centre of it. Engraved at the bottom of the crown are the words, made in China.

"If you're a princess then why don't you have on a crown like I do?" I mock, laughing to myself as I think about Candice boastfully modelling the cheap plastic tiara as if it were made of real gold and adorned with precious stones.

I head outside in search of Candice. For minutes I walk around the yard, manoeuvring through hordes of screaming, laughing children until finally I spot Candice walking by herself. In her hand is a small bouquet of red Roses. I call out to her and wave my hands frantically but she doesn't hear or see me. Picking up another Rose, Candice walks through a vine green door and enters one of Shariffe's garden houses. I tail her, following a trail of discarded Rose petals until I catch up to her. She is sitting on a large black rock beside a patch of yellow

Lilies. The bright yellow flowers give life to her green dress and dark skin.

"I am not a princess," she says sadly as she picks off a single Rose petal and throws it angrily to the ground.

"I am, I am a princess," she says happily as she picks off another petal and tosses it high into the air.

My heart wrenches and breaks into a million tiny pieces, there is only one Rose petal left. Candice frowns, her eyes swell with sadness and tears as she pulls off the last red petal and throws it to the ground.

"I," she sobs loudly. "I'm not a prin-"

"Your Majesty... Princess Royal Candice The First, you dropped your great, and wonderful crown of pure splendour," I scream, bowing my head in loving reverence, meanwhile tears flow uncontrollably from my eyes.

Stretching out my hands I offer the young princess back her prized tiara and at the same time I take back all of the horrible, untrue, things that I had said to her.

Candice's face fills with jubilee as she stares at me in disbelief. "You... You don't have to bow," she snickers, her large brown eyes flush with joy. "You're... You're a Princess too."

CHAPTER 18

(Vanessa)
****

I have been living with Shariffe for two months now and for the first time in my life, I am truly and completely happy. Losing myself within Shariffe has taught me that I don't need to get even with my family or the world or commit suicide to obtain peace, all I require is a genuine man who loves me unconditionally. I have been running from men my entire life, avoiding them as if they were poison, but now that I have decided to give myself to Shariffe I cannot imagine living my life without him. Men are integral pieces to a woman's happiness; love from a genuine man felt amazing and thrilling. Shariffe's love makes everyday of my existence worthwhile, his love gives me a reason for waking up each morning but most importantly his love forces me to love myself. And although I know that receiving his love means that I will eventually have to subject my physical body to the desires of his physical body I have decided that when that time comes I will not fight my feelings for Shariffe or allow my fears to consume me, I will allow him to have me without hesitation. Shariffe is a good man and if I have to give him my body in order to make him happy and make him love me then that is what I will do.

***

It has been a month and three days since I have fallen for Shariffe and during this time I have conformed completely to Shariffe's lifestyle. I have become his shadow, going and coming as he goes and comes, doing whatever he does. I garden with him, I clean and I cook and maintain the yard with him. I go for walks with him even when my monthly visitor arrives and my feet are swollen and sensitive. I drink his green concoctions and Ital vegetable soups, I jog and I hike, I read and I study, and I do all of these things without complaining.

Perfectly mimicking Shariffe's lifestyle has completely changed my life, I have shed all of my excess fat and I am no longer *overweight*, my body is toned and curvaceous. I am the *perfect* weight; I am slim in all of the right places and fat in all of the right places. My short, dull, hair has grown long and healthy looking and my skin now glows with new life. Yet, despite a complete overhaul of my former self, Shariffe continues to treat me and look at me as though I am only a friend but I can feel he and I growing closer and closer with each passing day.

I know he desires me, I can feel it in my heart, but for some strange reason he refuses to make the first move. Every moment that he is near me I want nothing more than to fall into him and have him cradle me in his loving, muscular, arms but my mother taught me that, *'A man should always make the first move, a lady must be pursued or she will never be appreciated.'*

Although, I hate my mother and her philosophies I accept that she knows far more about men than I do, so I submit to her... I will wait patiently for Shariffe to make the first move but maybe I can somehow speed up the whole process while still keeping my feelings hidden.

CHAPTER 19

ACCIDENT
(Vanessa)

You are not an accident. You are a precise presentation of
perfection and you have been placed here for a purpose. Your
birth was the beginning of something beautiful and don't you
ever forget that.

-

"Thou hast covered me in my mother's womb. I will praise
thee; for I am fearfully and wonderfully made: marvellous are
thy works; and that my soul knoweth right well."

Psalms 139:13-14
****

As usual, the kitchen is spotless, pristine and slowly filling with
the sweet aroma of cooked food. Like a mad chef, intoxicated
by the idea of preparing the perfect meal, Shariffe is running
around, stirring pots, chopping vegetables, blending fruits and
seasoning fish. Sitting down at the kitchen table, I flip eagerly
through the pages of a men's fitness magazine that I found in
one of the living rooms. I search the magazine until I find
exactly what I'm looking for. On page twenty-three there is a
beautiful olive skinned Brazilian male model.

I scream out, "Look at those arms, those legs, that chest
and those eyes. Oh my gosh he has such a nice butt, he has
to be the most attractive man I've ever seen. What do you
think, Shariffe?"

Lifting the magazine high into the air I dangle the picture as
bait in hopes of either making Shariffe wildly jealous or
uncovering the truth as to why he has not made the first move
on me but Shariffe doesn't respond. Instead, he continues
cooking and cleaning, paying the magazine and I no attention.
I close the magazine and drop it on the kitchen table.

"Shariffe, I really need to ask you something," I say, each of
my words infused with fear, bravery and uncertainty.

"Ask away," he says, while placing a bowl of hot food on the table next to two glass cups filled to the brim with thick, bright, pinkish purple liquid and a pot of boiled water for tea.

"Do you promise to answer honestly?

"Of course," he nods his head. "Is something wrong?"

"Are you gay?" I blurt out. "I know that it is none of my business but I need to know. I won't judge you, I swear."

"Yes."

"Yes, what?"

"Yes, I'm gay," his voice is monotonous and seems to lack any concern for just how important and devastating his answer is to me.

"Oh ok... Well... that explains everything," I sulk, my voice overflowing with disappointment. "How long have you been..." My throat knots as I struggle to finish my question. "That way?"

"You mean gay?"

"Yes," I nod my head in dismay.

"You can say the word, I'm not ashamed of who I am."

"Fine, how long have you been gay?"

He pauses and I can see from the happy star gazed look in his eyes and the wide smirk on his face that he is reliving the experience of his first intimate interaction as a gay man.

I look down at myself.

I'm wearing a white V-neck sweater with revealing black leggings. I wonder if seeing my body outlined and exposed through my clothes repulses him.

"I've been gay for just over two years."

"Two years! So you were gay when we first met?"

He nods his head, "you actually made me gayer and I thank you for that."

Wow!! I feel insulted and I wish I could put a bag over my face and just lie in a hole and die.

"So, I guess you have a boyfriend then?" A depressing wave of air tides from my mouth as I fight to hold back my tears.

"No," he shakes his head. "I don't."

"What! Why not?" I ask in shock. "Look at you, you're tall, you're handsome, you're rich, you're smart and you're nice. A man would be a fool not to want you... A woman would be a fool not to want you. I'm going to find you a boyfriend."

"Umm... Thanks... I guess," he laughs. "But Vanessa, I don't date men."

"I don't understand. How can you be gay if you don't date men?"

"Gay comes from the Old French word 'gai' and it means to be full of joy," he smiles cornily.

I discreetly release a much-needed sigh of relief but continue to stare at Shariffe seriously, "Have you ever slept with a man, been attracted sexually to a man or ever thought about pursuing a sexual relationship with a man?"

"No, I haven't."

"Are you sure?"

"Yes, I'm sure."

"Shariffe, it's ok with me if you have, I won't judge you. You don't have to lie to me, you can be the real you around me."

He smiles, "Well, it's good to know that you won't judge me and that I don't have to lie to you and that I can be the real me around you. But I'm not gay in the way you're thinking."

"Why aren't you married? Why don't you have your own kids and why do you treat me the way you do?"

"I'm not married because I never wanted to get married until I became gay."

"Shariffe, please stop joking around, this is important to me. I'm being serious with you."

"So am I," he says. "It wasn't until I was filled with the joy of the Holy Spirit that I was able to see and accept just how precious marriage truly is. Before I accepted Jesus I saw marriage as a form of self-handicap. My mentality was why should a tall, attractive, wealthy man like me get married and settle for one woman? One woman who would spend my money, waste my precious time and then eventually grow old and physically unattractive when I could be single, and free to always have a new, younger and prettier woman whenever I wanted.

It was a horrible mindset and I'm ashamed that I ever thought that way. I hurt a lot of women because of that mentality. It was only through accepting and maturing in God's concept of love did I learn that we have to love others and ourselves beyond the flesh. The shell of a person isn't the end all, it is what's on the inside that matters. When we love

beyond the flesh it makes it possible to truly become one with another individual, it makes it possible to see your spouse as precious and beautiful even when their flesh grows old and wrinkly. Loving beyond the flesh is the only way to truly love."
'Love beyond the flesh,'... His words echo in my head and shoot straight to my heart.

I think about Andrew and how his love for me stopped at my flesh. When I had started eating junk food, to gain weight, it was because I knew how much Andrew despised fat people. I wanted Andrew to stop touching me physically, I never wanted him to stop loving me or caring for me. But his love and care receded as my body expanded.

"Now that you've seen the light why don't you get married and have your own children?"

"I just can't, I want to," he says in a burst of emotion before taking a deep breath and calming back down. "Vanessa, marriage requires a lot of things that I cannot provide. I want to serve and love my wife, I want to fulfil all of her needs but if I get married right now I would only end up causing my wife more pain than joy," he sighs. "I really want a family Vanessa... but I just can't and if you don't mind I'd rather not speak about this right now."

I want to know more about the pain that he could inflict on the woman who he marries, I want to tell him that I am willing to experience that pain if it means I can be with him forever, but instead of saying these things I nod my head and respect his wishes.

The oven beeps, breaking the awkward silence.

He walks away from the kitchen table, puts on a pair of pink gloves that he purchased for breast cancer awareness month, and then takes out a tray of green Kale and Spinach muffins and sets them on the stovetop to cool.

They smell delicious.

He walks back to the table and sits down.

We both glance at the food on the table.

"We will reheat everything once we finish speaking. So, what is wrong with the way that I am treating you?" He asks.

"Nothing, you treat me great, you treat me better than anybody has ever treated me, I've never felt... love? like this... but I've lost so much weight and I just thought that maybe... You know what," I laugh while shaking my head. "Never mind, just forget I ever brought it up."

"No," Shariffe insists. "Love is a necessary component of life but the ways in which we need to be loved vary from person to person. We all need to be loved in different ways and if I am not loving you in the way that you need to be loved then please let me know so that I can change and love you correctly."

His dark brown eyes are fixed on me and I can see in them all the signs of genuine care and love.

I fight past my fears and insecurities and speak candidly, "I just thought that now that I'm skinnier and prettier that you would treat me different."

"Different how? Different why?"

"I'm not sure, I just know that I want more of you. I changed my entire life for you but you still treat me like I'm the same fat, pathetic, ugly girl that you met at the grocery store. I don't eat junk food, I workout with you, I cook and read with you, I spend all of my time with you, I clean with you, I do everything... a wife or girlfriend would do but you treat me... you treat me like a friend."

"I see..." he rubs his forehead and gazes off into space.

"That's all you have to say?"

He sighs, "We are friends Vanessa, so I treat you, and I love you as a friend. I never for one moment thought you were ugly or fat and I never judged you or withheld my love from you because of your weight or your physical appearance. Vanessa, I don't care how you look, I just want you to be healthy and happy. I didn't ask you to come live with me so that I could have access to your body or so that I could manipulate you and build myself a wife."

Tears gather at the backs of my eyes.

Shariffe lowers his head, "Vanessa, I need you to understand that its not you its me, I'm the problem. My whole life I've always been the problem and I know you won't believe me when I say this but I'm doing the right thing for you by only being your friend. I would hurt you if I loved you the way you want me to love you and I refuse to hurt you."

"How would you hurt me?"

"Vanessa, I don't want to talk about this," he says snappishly. "I'm not the man for you, I'm not your husband and that's that, end of discussion. Stop focusing on me and start focusing on God's love for you," his voice is sharp, direct, harsh, brash, hurtful and insensitive. "If it wasn't for Jesus and for Candice I would have never ever spoken to you, I-" he stops speaking abruptly, releases a long sigh while shaking his head.

Tears begin to gather at the backs of my eyes.

"Vanessa, forgive me, I-"

"Prove it!" I try to yell but my voice comes out as nothing more than a cracked weak squawk.

"Pardon?"

I inhale, successfully clearing my throat of as much pain as possible, "God, him, her, whatever you call it. I want you to prove to me right now that it exists and that it is what is *forcing* you to be nice to me," I say loudly.

"Vanessa, you're taking what I said the wrong way, I didn't mean it like that."

"How else am I supposed to take it?!" I yell. "If it weren't for God or for Candice you wouldn't have given me the time of day. God is somehow forcing you to talk to me, so prove it. Prove to me that God exists."

"Vanessa, all I meant is that if it weren't for God's love I wouldn't be able to appreciate you. The man I once was didn't appreciate anything or anyone, not even himself. If God didn't change me and show me the error of my ways and the perfection of His ways I would still be submitting to those errors, I would still be ruled by my blindness and directed by my misguided heart. I can see now Vanessa," he smiles while staring lovingly into my eyes. "And I spoke to you because I can see all that you are. Don't be offended if a blind man can't see you, I was blind Vanessa that's all I was saying. I was by no means implying that I was somehow better than you."

"So now you can see because God gave you sight?"

"Yes."

"Well, I want you to prove it."

"I can't prove to you that God exists, Vanessa. That's not my job or my goal."

I laugh mockingly, trying to mask my pain, "In other words you believe in something that you can't see or prove exists. Doesn't that make you crazy?"

"I see, hear and feel God all of the time Vanessa. And God proves His existence to different people in different ways. What it takes to convince me won't be the same as what it will take to convince you or any other human, which is why God has retained that responsibility for Himself. So, I'm not trying to prove the existence of God I'm just living my life and conducting myself in away that honours what I know to be the truth.

And as far as proof, for me, the existence of life, humans, animals, insects, trees and flowers, bacteria, the earth, the stars, thoughts, and emotions, good and evil are all proof that God exists. I don't believe that *nothing* existed and then magically *something* exploded from that nothing or that the universe as we know it was created so intricately and beautifully by accident. I don't believe that I was created by accident and I most certainly don't believe that you were created by accident, Vanessa."

My face shows every ounce of pain that is eating away at me and destroying me on the inside, but Shariffe doesn't care enough about me to notice. He doesn't love me enough to see every subtle expression of hurt that flows blatantly from every part of me towards him.

All he cares about is proving that his god is real.

I open my mouth to respond but before I can speak my mother begins to scream and yell at me. She tells me to shut up, she tells me to believe what he tells me to believe, she tells me to be a good and obedient little woman and not to do anything that will make him throw me out of his big fancy house. She tells me if I want to be loved by a man I have to learn how to keep quiet and submit.

"Never mind Shariffe, you don't get it."

"Then help me get it. I want to understand."

"No you don't, Shariffe!" I yell. "You don't want to understand, you don't want to get it! I've been trying to make you understand for the last month but you don't care! You don't care about me!"

"Vanessa, I do care," he sighs. "Please, help me understand."

"I don't care about your God," I snap. "Or proving that he exists, finding Jesus Christ won't make me happy. I'm already happy with the way that things are right now. I'm happy with you. I don't want any of God, I just want all of you!"

Not wanting him to see me cry I get up from around the table and exit the kitchen as quickly as I can.

Shariffe doesn't chase after me or call out to me. I wish he would but he never chases me, he always gives me my space but sometimes space hurts, sometimes space is the last thing that I need or want. Sometimes I need him close even when I'm pushing him away, sometimes I need to hear his voice even when I want him to shut up. Sometimes I wish he would force his love, sympathy and consideration on me instead of waiting for me to willingly walk into it.

When I arrive upstairs I notice that Shariffe has left his room door ajar.

He never leaves his door open.

A voice in my head flares up and begins to ask questions that it knows I can't answer unless I enter Shariffe's room and snoop around.

I stop moving, steady my breathing, and listen carefully to ensure that Shariffe isn't climbing up the long flight of wooden stairs to come and speak with me.

I hear the water from the kitchen sink begin to run.

He's washing dishes?!

That inconsiderate jerk is washing dishes? We just had an argument. I poured out my entire heart to him. I emptied myself in front of him, I was crying like a hurt little child and now he is downstairs washing dishes? I'm feeling naked, embarrassed, dirty and stupid and he is cleaning forks and spoons and pots and pans!

Like a raging bull, rushing angrily towards a wounded and vulnerable matador, I storm towards his room door and shove it wide open. The white door screams and groans, filling the once silent hallway with noise.

Before turning to flee I glance inside of Shariffe's room. His room is significantly smaller than mine and hanging just above his bed is a large, framed, photo of Candice. In the picture she is sitting on the lap of a caramel skinned, curly haired, woman. So that's her, that's his type.

She looks nothing like me.

Her hair is long and silky, her nose is straight, and she is skinny, really skinny.

She looks beautiful, I think as I slam my room door shut.

***

Thirty minutes later, after he has finished cleaning the kitchen, finished watering the household plants, finished feeding the dogs, Shariffe knocks on my room door.

"What do you want?" I shout from behind my room door.

"Andrew is on the phone. He says that he really needs to speak with you, it's urgent."

I open my room door, rip the cell phone from his hand, check the number in the call display and then end the call.

"How do you know him? I thought you said that you didn't know him."

"I don't know him."

"Then why does he have your number?"

"He was the old man with the bible at the hospital. I gave him one of my business cards. I didn't know his name was Andrew nor did I know you were avoiding him."

"What did he tell you about me?"

"He didn't tell me anything and I didn't ask anything... But Vanessa," his voice softens. "Something horrible is going to happen if you don't speak with Andrew, and forgive him."

"I don't care what happens to him."

"Vanessa, I never said that something horrible is going to happen to him. I said that something horrible is going to happen, I don't know who it is going to happen to, but you can prevent it by helping him."

"I refuse to help or forgive him, end of story," I say, mimicking Shariffe's cruel idiom.

"You can't help yourself and you can't help me if you don't know how to forgive. Your bitterness will spread from you over

to the children and I can't... I won't allow that to happen. I have to protect them no matter what, even if it means losing you."
His words hurt more than they should.
"That's fine!" I shout. "Since you see me as some kind of disease that will pollute your perfect, holy, life then I'll leave right now. Drive me back to the city and then leave me alone, forever."
"Vanessa," his voice remains cool and lax. "I care about you more than I can express and I am only asking you to go and speak with him because I know that it will help you. Your pain and your hate for him are spilling over into other parts of your life and causing you to miss out on a lot of the opportunities that Jesus would like you to take advantage of. Your pain almost prevented the two of us from getting to know one another," he glances down the hallway at his open door and then looks back and smiles at me. "Pain will cause us to make wrong decisions that will only cause us more pain. I want you to be happy Vanessa but true happiness does not come with baggage, you have to let it all go. Please, talk to him," he says softly, his voice tugging on the most compassionate parts of my being and activating them.
I turn and look away from him.
He has mastered the rare and delicate art of polite persuasion. He understands how to use his words to soften my heart and convince me to do all of the things that I don't want to do. He knows how to attack me without being aggressive or hurtful. He knows how to ignore his ego and fight with his love, and when he attacks me with his love he will always defeat me, I will always submit to him because it is impossible to fight or resist the unrelenting love of the one whom you love. The right words from the right person are powerful, they can penetrate the stoniest of hearts.
"Fine, I'll do it, Shariffe. I'll go and see him... for you."

CHAPTER 20

REVENGE

(Vanessa)

You must forgive, even though it may be hard to forget, even
though it may be difficult to move on, even though the pain
may be present for the rest of your life
you must forgive.

-

*"Repay no one evil for evil ... "if your enemy is hungry, feed
him; if he is thirsty, give him something to drink; Do not be
overcome by evil, but overcome evil with good."*

Romans 12:17-21
****

A young child is standing in front of me. She is wearing a red
shirt, bright pink shorts, and a black baseball cap. By the look
of her face and the size of her body she is no more than
eleven years old. An eerie feeling passes through me as I
stare at her. I want to pull her in close and tell her everything I
know about the man who resides at the house she is standing
in front of. I want to warn her, I want to beg her to be careful, I
want to tell her not to talk to strangers no matter how nice they
may seem. I open my mouth to speak to the little girl when
another thought enters my mind. This thought scolds me, it
tells me that I am not the child's mother and that I have no
right to parent children who are not my own, I have no right to
disfigure the mind's of innocent ignorant children just because
I am a paranoid, bitter, wreck of a woman.

I submit to the other thought.

I purse my lips and watch as the child reaches into her
oversized yellow carrier bag and withdraws a rolled up bundle
of newspapers. The little girl pitches the roll of papers as hard
as she can at the navy blue door. The newspaper sails through

the air twisting and twirling over a dozen times before crashing with a loud thud against the door. "Yes! I did it! I finally got it! Right in the middle!" The little girl boasts before running to the next house and repeating the process.

I turn away from the little child and focus all my attention on the navy blue door that is now slowly opening. The man who emerges from inside the house looks nothing like the large, barrel chested, monster that I remember from my childhood. The creature that I now see before me is wrinkled, sickly, and weak looking.

I smirk to myself.

Today, I will have my revenge.

CHAPTER 21

DENIAL

(Andrew)

-

To live in denial is to submit to darkness, to glorify our indignations, to put our own destruction on a pedestal and praise it as though it were a virtue.

****

Everything around me slows to a halt. The sunshine, the air, the birds chirping, all the common phenomena of life that normally fill my front yard are nullified under the radiant glory of her presence.

"Ang... Angel...?" her nickname exits my mouth in a welded cacophony of sweet joy and sour regret.

I squint and rub my eyes in disbelief while walking to the edge of my porch.

"Vanessa," I yell, my voice cracking under the weight of the moment.

She stands at the foot of my lawn staring at me, her face showing neither signs of anger or joy.

"Vanessa," I beg while reaching out to her from the edge of my porch. "I'm so sorry... please... Angel. Please, come inside, we need to talk."

She looks me up and down and furrows her eyebrows in contempt.

"Please," I plead once more, my voice heavy with yearning and desperation. "I'm sorry, Vanessa, I'm so sorry for everything I did to you but please... we need to talk. Please! Please, come inside."

***

As I lead her to the family room I can feel the cold hate filled glare of her eyes piercing through me. I deserve to be hated, I deserve to be crucified and punished, I deserve to receive the murderous intent that is swelling in her heart for me but I also deserve her forgiveness and her redemption, I am no longer the same man who hurt her so many years ago. I made a mistake but I have been reborn, I am a new and better man.

Vanessa sits down on a medium sized white chair and folds her arms in contempt before scanning the room with her eyes.

I cringe with concern.

There are no pictures of her on any of the walls or tables. I didn't want to remove all of her pictures from the house but I had to. Her pictures were reminders of what I had done, reminders of my great mistake, reminders that were preventing me from being a new and better man. Her pictures were caging me to my old ways.

"We're going to be renovating soon so I removed a lot of the pictures, I am going to put them back up after the renovation is complete."

She leans forward in her chair and continues to wander the living room with her eyes, entering spaces that I wish I could lock her out of.

"Where is my mother?"

"She's not here."

"I didn't ask where she isn't, I asked where she is."

"Your sister is in Florida on a volleyball scholarship. Your mother is out there visiting her. To be honest," I sigh. "I don't see your mother too often anymore, things have not been the best between us since you left."

"Have you told her? Does she know what you did to me?"

"Yes, of course she knows, I told her everything. I've confessed my sins, Angel... I mean Vanessa."

"What did she say?"

"She cried, she blamed herself, she said that she had failed you and was a horrible mother and then she threatened to call the police and have me arrested. I told her that I had betrayed her trust and I was the only failure in this whole situation. I told her that I deserved to go to jail and that if she chose to call the police I would tell them the truth about what I had done, and I would accept my punishment but your mother is such a forgiving woman. Months later, your mother came to me and told me that she had seen Jesus Christ in a dream and He told her that I deserved to be forgiven."

She bites down on her bottom lip, releases a short burst of air from her nose and then says, "So Jesus told my mother that it was alright for you to rape me?"

"No, of course not!" I exclaim. "God would never consent or promote rape. God wanted your mother to live a life of forgiveness and love. God didn't want your mother's heart to be polluted by bitterness and hatred. Holding a grudge poisons the spirit. Everything can and should be forgiven, there are no big sins or small sins there are only opportunities to forgive and express love. Your mother is a strong woman, she saw an opportunity to love me beyond my faults and that was what she did."

My Angel breathes heavily and grinds her teeth. "So let me get this correct, a woman is strong if she continues to support and sleep with the man who raped her daughter?"

"No," I defend. "I'm not saying that."

"Sorry, I guess I misunderstood. Maybe what you're saying is that God views raping someone as identical to lying to someone or stealing candy from a store? If I killed you right now, if I grabbed your old wrinkly neck and just squeezed on it until you were lifeless, it would be the same as committing any other so called sin... right?"

I turn away from her and hang my head in shame. I close my physical eyes, open my spiritual heart and speak intimately to my God. I beg Him to intervene, I beg Him to fill my mouth with the right words.

"Jesus says that you are being spiritually attacked by demons," I say suddenly meanwhile opening my eyes and looking at her burdened face. "God wants to help you, you are special to Him and He wants to set you free from your anger and pain but first you must forgive me."

She laughs at my words.

I scan her entire body, searching for a point of weakness in which I can enter and influence her. She isn't wearing a wedding or an engagement ring I notice.

I smile within myself and then I attack.

"Jesus says," I speak with confidence, authority and a deep bass in my voice. "That the man who you are living with, the tall man with the long hair from the hospital, he is in love with you and he will marry you but only if you forgive me."

Her eyes open wide with hope and she half smiles, "He... he's my husband?"

"Yes, Vanessa, God says yes. He is your husband, he is in love with you but you must forgive me or he will not marry you."

"He's... He's in love with me?"

"Yes, Vanessa, yes."

"Jesus just told you all of this, right now?"

"Yes," I say quickly. "But you have to forgive me first."

"So Jesus is here, in this room, right now?"

"Yes. He is everywhere all of the time."

She shakes her head, her eyes filling with a mixture of hate and rage, "Was He there when you were raping me? Was He telling you what to say while you were raping me? Did He tell you to-" She stops speaking abruptly and gags.

I look down in disgust, "Vanessa, I don't want to live in the past, let's move forward."

Tears are running down her cheeks now, tears that would not exist if I were not such a disgusting filthy animal.

"Was He there?" She asks again.

"Vanessa we-"

"Answer my question," she screams. "I want to know if He was there. If your God was watching you rape me, and if He heard me when I was begging Him to save me. I want to know if the same God who you worshipped while you were raping me is the same God who is speaking to you right now!!"

"Yes," I digress.

"Say it," she commands, her cold eyes piercing my broken heart.

Sadness eats away at my insides and spreads like bacteria as I remember her screaming and clawing at me. I wanted to stop, I wanted so bad to stop but I couldn't. No matter how hard I tried or how loud she cried it was impossible for me to stop.

"Yes Vanessa," I cry. "Yes, God was there while I was raping you and yes Vanessa God heard you when you were asking Him to save you. And yes Vanessa it is the same God who is speaking to me right now."

"Did He tell you to rape me?"

"No," I protest. "It was Satan Vanessa. Satan made me do it."

"Did God tell Satan to tell you to rape me?"

"No," I shake my head fervently.

"Then who told Satan to tell you to rape me? Where did Satan get the idea to tell you to rape me? Who or what influences and controls Satan, who puts evil thoughts in Satan's head? Did Satan just get up one morning and say I want to rape and hurt and destroy people? Does Satan create his own thoughts, or do his thoughts come from somewhere, or someone else? Where did the thought of rape come from, which all-powerful being created that evil thought in Satan's head? If God created all things then he created rape, the ability to rape, the desire to rape, he created everything that is wrong with this world."

"Vanessa, the... the devil... it was the devil," I say, tongue tied beyond that.

"It was you Andrew!" She snaps loudly. "Stop all of this devil and God nonsense and just admit it. Take responsibility, I need you to take responsibility!" her voice cracks. "It wasn't some red man with horns and it wasn't some man sitting on a cloud. It was you! You raped me, you're the devil!" she screams. "And if your God is real why didn't he help me? Why didn't he kill you and save me, why did he let me die if he's such a good God? Why did he kill a little innocent child and allow a monster like you to go on living? Why did he let you hurt me? Why did you let yourself hurt me?" she cries. "You were supposed to protect me."

"I don't know Vanessa," I wipe my face clean. "I don't know, I don't know. I'm so sorry Angel," I weep aloud.

"I don't want your sorry."

"What do you want? Tell me what you want me to do. Whatever you ask I'll do it, I just want us to be a family again."

"I want you to admit that it was 'you' who raped me, you and nobody else," she exhales.

"Vanessa, it was Sata-"

"No," she interrupts. "Admit it was you or I am leaving right now and you will never see or hear from me again and I will never forgive you."

"I... I raped you Vanessa," the words burn like acid as they leak from my lips towards her ears. "It was me, I did it. No one influenced me. Not God, not satan. I did it."

She releases a heavy sigh, sits up straight and looks me dead in my eyes, "Thank you, I needed to hear you say that."

"You're welcome Ange... Vanessa, I just really want us-"

"No, no, we're not done yet," she chuckles, her eyes raw and polluted with a cold vindictiveness. "You raped me Andrew and nothing will ever erase that," she says, choking on her own words. "How much is my forgiveness worth to you?"

"What do you mean?"

"What are you willing to pay me for my forgiveness? How does forgiving you benefit me?"

"You'll get God and heaven and eternal life," I say.

She laughs, "I want something real, something that actually exists, something I can see... something that hurts you... really hurts you."

"But, but the bible says-"

"I don't care what the bible says," my Angel roars, her voice frothing with fire. "Do you do everything that ridiculous book tells you to do?"

"I try," a heavy sigh ebbs from my mouth. "I'm not perfect, Vanessa, but I try... I really do try."

"I have an idea," she exclaims, her face now glowing with excitement and joy. "Somewhere in your holy bible it says that if your right hand constantly causes you to do evil then you should cut it off. Right?"

I nod my head yes, "Matthew 5 verse 30."

"Was raping me evil?"

"Yes, but-"

Before I'm able to finish my sentence my Angel stands to her feet and walks from the living room to the kitchen. Less than a minute later she returns, sits back down, and drops a large butcher's knife on the coffee table in front of us.

"Cut it off, and then I'll forgive you."

"I don't understand."

"Cut off the thing that caused you to sin, do what your bible says and then I'll forgive you," she nudges the knife towards me.

"This isn't necessary," I sigh. "Jesus has healed me. I no longer have those dirty desires; I am a new and better man. You have to trust me."

"I don't trust you Andrew, and I won't forgive you unless I know for certain that you no longer have the ability to do what you did to me to anyone else. Cut it off. If you're a true Christian then cut if off."

"Leave my house, Vanessa."

"Excuse me?"

"Get out of my house," I growl.

She stares me down and folds her arms over her chest, "After what you did to me do you really think you can just throw me out? Cut it off or I will,' She growls back.

"I raped you!" I scream suddenly, my old voice rising with power and life. "Yes I did it, it was me. I made a mistake!" I sneer. "Should I spend my whole life paying for one mistake? Don't I deserve forgiveness? Doesn't everyone deserve forgiveness?"

"No," she grits her teeth. "People like you do not deserve forgiveness. When you steal something that can never be given back, when you break something that can never be fixed you... don't... deserve... forgiveness! Cut it off!" she commands.

"Get out!" I growl. "Or I will call the police and have you thrown out, Vanessa."

"You'll call the police?" she laughs. "Call them, I'll tell them everything you did."

"I'll deny it."

"I'll get my mother to vouch for me, she'll-"

"Your mother knows nothing," I interrupt with a yell.

"But... but you said that you told her," her face creases and folds with shock and dismay.

I shake my head and exhale, "It's called a lie Vanessa. I lied to you. I lied to you to try and protect you, I lied to you in order to spare your feelings but you don't want my lies, you don't want my protection, you want to feel the full force of the truth."

Tears roll from her red eyes. Oceans of emotions rising up from the depths of her soul, liquefying, and then rushing down her cheeks but I don't care anymore. A bitter, bratty little girl who refuses to forgive me despite the fact I have done everything in my power to be forgiven will not step all over me.

"Well here is the truth, Vanessa," I continue, staring without remorse into her tired and defeated eyes. "People are raped every day; men, women, children, even animals are raped, you're not the only one who has been raped. Get... over... it!" I yell. "We all go through pain, every person has been hurt. You're not special because you've been raped, you don't deserve special treatment because of it and I will no longer feel guilty for it, I said sorry and that is all you are going to get from me."

"Cut it off, please," she cries like the weak, little, vulnerable child that she is. "I need you to, I," she stumbles over her words then inhales a deep breath before clearing her throat. "Cut it off, Andrew, please. I'm begging you... I... please," she sobs. "I'll forgive you, I'll forgive you, just cut it off... please."

"No," I say, my voice firm and unapologetic. "I tried to help you Vanessa but you don't want to be helped, you want to live and die in your past, you want to cry over spilled milk instead of cleaning up the mess and pouring yourself another glass, you want to be pitied... well I'm not going to pity you... now get up and get out of my house," I snarl.

CHAPTER 22

DEVILS

(Vanessa)

Your downfall is the devil's greatest work of art. He will
beautify your mistakes and convince you to make more. He
will destroy you in the most ferocious and elegant way
possible.

-

"Be alert and of sober mind. Your enemy, the devil, prowls
around like a roaring lion looking for someone to devour."

1 peter 5:8
****

For years I fantasized about all of the horrible things that I
would do to him if I ever got the chance and when the chance
finally came I just sat there like a weak child and allowed him
to shout at me and throw me out of his house. Even as an old
feeble man he was still stronger than me, despite my age and
my knowledge he still defeated me.

Tears begin to pour from my eyes.

Why didn't I cut it off myself, why didn't I grab him by his old
wrinkly neck and run that silver blade right through his black
heart? Why didn't I kill him?

Why am I so weak?

*'Go back, it's not too late. Go back and give him what he
deserves,'* a soothing voice ricochets back and forth in my
mind.

"Why is such a beautiful woman crying?" A man's voice fills
my ears.

When I turn to my left there is a tall, clean-shaven, oval
shaped man in a sleek black suit standing there. Embarrassed,
I wipe my face clean and try to walk away from the man as
quickly as possible but he follows me and uses his pumpkin
shaped stomach to block my path.

"Who is he?" the man demands.

My forehead wrinkles in confusion.

"The man who hurt you, the piece of trash who made you cry," he continues. "Who is he? What's his name?" The man in black asks with such ferocity and girth that I feel compelled to answer.

"Umm," I sniffle. "His... his name is-"

"Stop," the man interrupts. "I don't care what his name is or who he is and neither should you. As far as you and I are concerned he no longer exists, he is dead to us," he declares with an authoritative wave of his hand before pulling open the large black door that he is standing in front of.

Loud, bass saturated, music flows out from the doors of the club and floods the city streets.

"Free for the next six! Free for the next six! Free for the next six," the oval shaped man screams.

Four beautiful women, one in a green dress, one in a blue dress, one in a pink dress and one in a yellow dress rush past me and the man in black and scurry into the nightclub. Two skinny black men, one wearing a skin-tight yellow shirt and the other wearing a red dress shirt, follow closely behind the women. The two men stop at the doorway and stare at the four women as they climb the long stairs leading into the club.

"I swear, I swear, I swear, I love, love, love!! Ethiopian women," exclaims the man in yellow. "I have never in my life seen an unattractive Ethiopian woman. Did you see the body on that one in the yellow dress? Oh, my gosh," the man in yellow begins to convulse, shaking his head and body as if possessed by some sensation that is too powerful for his small frame. "I have to get her number tonight, man's dem have to get her number tonight. I swear on my life, I am not leaving here tonight without her number."

The man in red laughs, "So I guess this is going to be your new home then?"

"Whatever, you're a haaaater bro," the man in yellow says in a high-pitched cartoonish voice. "But yo, real talk, *top left tingz*, I'm gonna get her number or DIE trying."

"Ethiopians only date other Ethiopians or white men," the man in red laughs.

"Women don't care about culture, race or religion. All women care about is money."

"Which you don't have."

"But she doesn't know that," the man in yellow laughs. "I have enough money to pretend to be rich for at least one week and believe me one week is all I need to make her fall in love."

"She'll know that you're broke and jobless when she finds out that you're still living with your parents and share a room with your little brother or when she sees the car that you don't drive. Don't you still sleep on a bunk-bed?"

"Listen, don't DISRESPECT bunk-beds. Bunk beds are just the smarter option for my CURRENT living arrangement; they save on space by making vertical use of my room. Also, I take the bus because I care about the environment. Global Warming is no joke fam, that's what killed the Dinosaurs and if it can kill Dinosaurs I'm sure it can kill humans... It's science."

The short man in red laughs a haughty laugh, "You know you're an idiot right? But because I love you like a brother, I'll do this for you, if you can get her number then you can use my condo and my car."

"I love you man, you're a true bredren. I don't care what your mom and dad say about you, you're a good guy," the man in yellow laughs in response.

The two men shake hands, hug, and then walk inside of the club.

"Believe me," the bouncer smiles. "A little dancing and a little liquor makes life a lot better. Tell the bartender that you're Ronell's friend and she'll make you feel better on my behalf."

I don't want to go inside the dark, loud, club. I want to go home to Shariffe, I want to curl up in his arms, escape in his warm embrace and fall asleep to the deep soothing sound of his voice but sadly Shariffe was too much of a self-righteous prude to ever allow any of these much needed things to happen. Instead of holding me, and comforting me, instead of kissing me and squeezing me, he would want to pray for me and develop a problem resolution strategy to reconcile Andrew and I.

"Listen to me," the man with the big belly says loudly. "Stop thinking about him and just go inside and get yourself a drink or two and find yourself a man," he laughs. "Find yourself a good man, a man who deserves you. You're a good woman and you deserve to be happy ... Yolo, right?"

"Yolo?"

"You Only Live Once."

The truth of his words mix intimately with my desires then blends perfectly with the slow pulsating music that is now flowing from inside of the club. The sign above his head emanates an inviting red glow.

I wipe my eyes and despite my true desires, I walk up the long black stairs and enter the club. The room is massive, hot, and smells of alcohol and marijuana smoke. I walk across the dance floor, manoeuvring my way around moving bodies until I arrive at the bar. I sit down on a leather barstool that holds my frame perfectly. Five months ago I could never have sat on this stool without making a fool of myself. Five month's ago the bouncer at the door would have ignored me.

The Bartender, a skinny white woman with short brown hair and her breasts hanging out, walks over to me. I mouth Ronell's name and the Bartender nods her head, smiles and winks at me before handing me a glow in the dark drink menu. I pick my poison and wait for it to arrive. Before I know it cherry and lemon flavoured liquor is running down my throat and slowly erasing the dark dingy world around me. After a few more glasses I feel myself floating towards the dance floor. I try to command myself to turn around and sit back down at the bar but my body ignores me and keeps moving forward until I'm lost in the crowd. The loud music falling from the speakers above my head flows relentlessly into my out of control body, rushing first to my waist and then my legs until my entire body is rocking and dipping wildly. My hands are high in the air swaying madly from left to right and I'm screaming at the top of my lungs. I don't know what I'm saying but I'm screaming and it feels amazing.

I feel weightless.

I feel free.

I feel happy, truly happy.

I love it!

Suddenly, the room goes pitch black, the music stops, everybody around me begins to scream and then seconds later a single bright red light begins to flick on and off rapidly. Up-tempo music crashes messily out of the speakers invigorating the people around me, causing them to move faster and rougher while grinding their pelvises on one another. Men grab hold of women, women grab hold of men, men grab hold of men, women grab hold of women, someone grabs hold of me.

"Hey beautiful," a man's deeply soothing voice enters my ears. "How about you allow me to buy you a drink?"

I can feel his lips brushing gently against the nape of my neck as he rhythmically controls the flow and ebb of my waist with the flow and ebb of his waist.

"Rooomell?" I slur as I pull away and turn around.

"No, no," the man laughs. "My name is Donovan but I can be Romell if you'd like and I can be Romeo if you'd really like."

The urge to run away and hide rises in me but the liquor speaks to my brain and convinces me that the unknown man is a friend, someone who can be trusted, someone who will make me happier than Shariffe ever could.

"So how about that drink? What are you having?"

"U'mm nat thursy..."

"Then let me make you thirsty," he smiles.

Grabbing hold of my waist, he pulls me into him and then turns me around. I can feel his large fingers pressing deep into my flesh, massaging parts of me that he shouldn't be massaging. I want to push him away but the liquor hits me, killing my desire to break free.

Thirty minutes later, I'm sweaty and I'm thirsty.

Donovan grabs my right hand and charges, like a raging bull, through the crowd of dancing people. He pushes men and women out of his path. Nobody stands in his way or dares to say anything to him as he bulldozers over whomever he chooses.

He is so powerful.

Donovan is a real man.

I could never imagine Shariffe doing something so dominant, so bold, so masculine. Despite how large and muscular Shariffe is he is still very frail, like a little boy. He is always tripping over his own feet, and things are always slipping out of his hands and breaking on the floor. Donovan is a real man. His grip feels strong and secure like nothing could ever slip from it.

Donovan and I sit down at the bar and he orders drinks for the both of us.

I can't stop myself from staring at him.

He is beautiful and majestic.

His skin is ruddy and refined yet rough and hardened.

His facial features are strong and chiselled.

He is muscular and tall.

His teeth are pristine and white.

He looks just like Shariffe but a million times better and without those stupid, ugly, dirty, smelly, dreads.

I hate dreads.

I hate Shariffe.

I hate Shariffe for having dreads.

For the rest of the night, amidst sips of cold tangy alcohol, Donovan and I have the most lovely and interesting conversations. Donovan doesn't believe in God, he believes in the fluidity of love and life, he believes in the cosmic power of the universe. He believes that we create our own world and that the universe is nothing more than a ball of endless possibilities that can be vehemently influenced by our desires. He respects women, he loves children, and best of all he loves and he accepts me for me... the real me.

Donovan is the defender of my truth.

Like a flower, powerless against the warmth and light of the sun's rays, I open up to Donovan and reveal all the secrets that I possess. Amidst tears and drunken slurs I tell him all about Andrew; I tell him all the things that I could never tell a high-minded, judgemental, man like Shariffe.

Upon hearing my life story Donovan sighs in pain, grimaces in disgust, and slams his massive fists against the bar counter almost breaking the black marble counter in half. He apologizes to me on behalf of all men for what Andrew has done to me. He says that women represent the creative energy of the universe and deserve to be respected and honoured as manifested goddesses. He wishes he could change the world so that women would be cherished but sadly the universe is filled with others who use the vibrations of the universe for evil and manipulation. He will never manipulate or use me because his portion of the universe is a place of love, peace, truth and acceptance. He tells me that Andrew is an animal who doesn't deserve my forgiveness; he needs to be removed from the universe. He offers to go to war on my behalf, to beat Andrew to a bloody pulp, to completely erase his negative vibrations so that they don't infect another living soul. I want to say yes, I want to cheer on my brave warrior, I want Donovan to protect me and defend my honour but for some strange stupid reason I say no.

"Last Call! Last Call! Last Call!!!" The Bartender screams, her voice some how rising over the deafening music.

Donovan orders more drinks and hands them to me. Shariffe doesn't drink, he is so uptight and boring, he doesn't know how to have a good time. Shariffe is like a 90-year-old man who is trapped in a 30-year-old man's body, all Shariffe does is cook, clean, garden, workout, and take care of the children at his day camp... he doesn't do anything exciting and fun, he doesn't live life.

Suddenly, an image of Shariffe smiling at me with his hands outstretched creeps past the wall of liquor. I hear him calling my name, telling me that I should come home to him so that he and I can be friends forever.

My eyes begin to water.

I want to go home to Shariffe but I want more than friendship. I glance at Donovan hoping to receive some semblance of comfort but all of his appeal has left him. His perfect smile is gone, and his large tank like body has withered to nothing. I grab my glass and take a large gulp. The skinny, strange looking, man with big ears sitting in front of me disappears and Donovan's chiselled muscles, his barrelled chest and his beautiful face return to me. I take another shot of liquor and Shariffe disappears, pushed to the back of my mind where he belongs.

Donovan raises his hand to my face and gently wipes away my tears before handing me another drink. I swallow the shot of liquor and stare aimlessly into Donovan's warm, welcoming, hazel eyes.

He hands me another drink.

The music stops playing.

The room goes black and the beautiful bright red light begins to flicker again.

I place the small glass to my lips and pour the contents down my throat.

I feel Donovan's fingers sliding slowly up my thigh.

'*You Only Live Once,*' *Donovan says before leaning forward and pressing his soft lips against mine.*

CHAPTER 23

SHAME
(Vanessa)

We all make mistakes, we all have done things that we would like to keep hidden, we all need to forgive and be forgiven.
-
"Be ye kind one to another, tender hearted, forgiving one another, even as God for Christ's sake hath forgiven you."

Ephesians 4:32
****

My head is pounding and I can feel the contents of my stomach trying to escape through my mouth. I inhale a breath of fresh air before burrowing myself deep into my plush white covers, hiding from all light and sound. I feel horrible, I feel like I am going to die, the only thing that is keeping me alive is the fact that I know Shariffe will make everything better. Soon he will knock on my room door, serve me warm ginger tea, a hot breakfast and then he and I will head to the sunroom to watch the sunrise

Sheltered under my warm sheets I wait for my Shariffe to arrive. I count down in my head from 10 to 0 but the strangest thing happens. When I reach 0 there is no musical knock or baritone voice emanating from my room door.

He's late... but he's never ever late.

I roll over to check the exact time on the clock on my nightstand. Screaming as loud as I can I scurry from my bed, grab whatever clothes I can find and get dressed as quickly as possible.

"Leave!" I yell at the half naked stranger lying in my bed. "You have to get out right now, right now out! Get up, and get out! Get out!"

"Wha? Why, why you yelling?" the man stirs awake and looks up at me.

"You have to leave," I cry out, my emotions swirling within me. "You have to go right now! Get your things and get out!" He sits up, allowing his back to rest sluggishly on my headboard meanwhile unashamedly exposing his malnourished chest, his pumpkin belly, and his two chicken legs, "Is wha wrong?" Why me have to leave?"

"Nothing is wrong. I... You... You just have to leave..." I say hastily. "I... I have to go to work."

"Work?" he hisses in a thick Jamaican accent. "Don't worry bout work, I cyan stay here till you come bock."

"Listen to me carefully," my voice stern and packed with aggression. "I want you to get dressed and get out of my house right now! Oh my gosh," I almost cry out of disgust. "Get out of my bed! Get out of my bed! Get off of my sheets! Eeewwww!

"Eww? Is what you mean eww? Is disrespect you a try disrespect Donovan?" he says, standing to his feet and completely exposing his gangly, misshapen, body.

"No, no," I accidently glance down at his worm then cringe and turn away. "Listen, I'm... I'm sorry if I'm coming off as rude but I have a busy day today. I have to got to work and then right after work I am... I'mmm... I'm going straight to my mother's house to take care of her... sheeee... she's sick."

He hisses at me again and then sits his naked body back onto my bed.

I want to vomit.

"Why you never did just tell me that from di beginning? Mi is sorry fi hear bout you madda. Is what sicken she?"

"What did you say?"

"You nuh understand English? Mi say, is what sickness your madda have? Is what she sick wid?"

"Cancer... She has cancer," I lie, but I wish my lie were true. I really, really, wish it were true. She deserves cancer. I wish she could get every type of cancer in the world. I wish everybody else's cancer would leave their bodies and enter my mother's body. "Now can you please get dressed so that we can leave? Please, I don't want to be late for work."

After a few more minutes of going back and forth and after promising him that I would call him once I leave my mother's house, I am finally able to convince him to leave. He dips down, picks up his clothes from off my bedroom floor and then walks into my bathroom and shuts the door behind him. Seven, excruciatingly long, minutes later he finally re-emerges. He is wearing black skinny jeans and a white short-sleeved dress shirt and a bright red plastic watch. Without saying a word to him, I tow him downstairs as quickly as possible. Standing impatiently by the front door, I wait forty-five seconds while he puts on a pair of light brown suede boots. When he finally finishes, I rush out the front door with him, forgetting to put on my own shoes in the process. While stepping shoeless through the tall green grass, of Shariffe's front yard, I feel something warm flatten under the weight of my foot. When I glance behind me, I see the mangled remains of a bird's body surrounded by a mess of bright red feathers. I look down; there is blood, guts, and feathers sticking to the sole of my right foot. I want to vomit, I want to scream and cry, I need to stop walking and clean my foot but more than anything else in the world I need to get Donovan out of the mansion before Shariffe sees him.

The car lot is only twenty-feet away and from the car lot to the front gate it is a short ten-second drive.

"Good morning Vanessa and Vanessa's friend! How are the both of you doing, today?" Shariffe yells from some location in the yard.

My heartbeat quickens at the sound of his voice but I pretend not to hear him. He screams my name again, fighting for my attention, but I continue to ignore him and increase my speed. Suddenly, Donovan grabs me by the hand, stopping me dead in my tracks.

"Who is dat?"

"He's nobody, he's just my Gardener. Now, let's go," I say in haste.

"Him nuh look like Gardna," he says while slanting his eyes and staring directly at Shariffe.

"Vanessa!" Shariffe yells. "Is everything all right over there? Do you need my help?"

I continue to ignore Sharrife, I'm too ashamed to look at him or acknowledge him in anyway but from the corner of my eyes I can see him rushing towards me with a large knife in his hand.

"Donovan, can we go please?"

"No," Donovan declares. "I want to know who he is because he doesn't look like a gardener."

I need to get out of here but I have no idea what to do or say to convince Donovan to leave. Suddenly, my mother rises in my mind and tells me exactly what I need to do and say. I don't want to listen to her but I know that she is an expert when it comes to these types of situations.

"Can we please go now baby?" I ask softly. "I don't want to be late for work and I ... I want to... I want to finish in the car what we started last night in my room and I want you to drive my Lexus while I focus on making you happy. But we have to leave right now.... Like right, right now."

Thinking about him touching me is more disgusting than the bird guts on my foot bottom.

I fake smile at him.

He smiles, and then follows me like an obedient dog to Shariffe's Lexus.

When I glance back Shariffe has stopped walking towards me and is standing in position like a war ready soldier, staring intently at the man and I. The dark, angry, and murderous look that covered Shariffe's face while he was storming towards the Donovan and I has now evaporated. He smiles at me, and waves bye.

I look away from him, unlock the car door, sit in the driver's seat and then signal for him to go around and sit in the passenger's seat.

"Mi think you say a mi ago drive so you could finish what you start last night."

Just shut up and get in the car you stupid fool, because of you Shariffe probably thinks I'm some cheap floozy.

"As soon as we get out of the yard," I wink.

This time I actually do vomit a little, but I swallow it back before it can leave my mouth.

Donovan smiles at me and then walks around to the front passenger's side door where he enters the car and sits down.

I look at him and cringe. I can't believe he was in my bed, he was inside of me, he was kissing me, he was holding me.

What is wrong with me?

What is happening to me?

I'm doing all of the things that I promised myself I would never do.

I'm becoming just like my mother. This is all Shariffe's fault; he created this version of me, this weak, needy, constantly compromising version of me.

My entire body is shaking with anger as I drive towards downtown. Taking Simcoe road route 88 I merge onto Highway 400 South, then merge onto the 401 West, then transfer to the 427 South where I take the Gardner Expressway East. I drive around Toronto, keeping Donovan at bay with seductive winks, moans and empty promises until I find Club Eros. In the light of the day the brown building looks cheap, and raunchy. It looks like a place where you would go to find sleazy men like Donovan, it looks like a place where you would go if for some strange reason you wanted to get a S.T.D.

I will have to go get checked by a doctor.

I pull into the empty lot, park the car, and then unlock all the doors.

Donovan turns towards me, "Mi think we did ago-"

"I don't want to mess up the leather," I interrupt. "Do you mind if we do it in your car or somewhere outside?"

I feel disgusted with myself, but the way I'm acting is necessary.

'Men are sexual beings. If you want to control him you have to make him think that sex is a possibility. Dangle it in front of him,' my mother instructs.

I wonder how Shariffe would respond to me if I acted like this with him. Would he obey me as well? Is this what I have to do to get the man I love? Do I have to completely sacrifice who I am and become the woman who I hate? Can all men be controlled by the prospect of sex?

I wink at Donovan, lick my bottom lip, and slowly but seductively open my car door.

He smiles at me, opens his door, gets out of Shariffe's Lexus, closes the door behind him and begins to skip and run happily towards his car.

I quickly slam my door shut, push the ignition button, throw my car in drive and speed off as fast as I can.

When I arrive back at the mansion, I avoid Shariffe and sneak up to my room. My room windows are wide-open allowing sunlight to enter and new spotless white sheets have been neatly spread on my bed.

I sigh, close my blinds and fall onto my bed.

"He'll never want me now," I cry.

CHAPTER 24

DEPRAVITY

(Andrew)

Your mind is like a body of water and every action, good or
bad, is like a substance that mixes with and alters the state of
your water. You have the ability to pollute or purify your
drinking supply.

-

God shows his love for us in that while we were still sinners,
Christ died for us.

Romans 5:8
****

Staggering over to my window, I use my index finger and my
thumb to discretely spread apart my white blinds.
    I stare into the streets, waiting patiently for her to arrive.
    She is late today.
    Today, I will invite her inside.
    I will offer her a cool glass of water and something
nutritious to eat, something to rehydrate and nourish her tired
body from the burdens of carrying around a heavy bag of
newspapers all day in the boiling hot sun.
    Today, I will help her.
    I am a good man.

CHAPTER 25

HELP

(Vanessa)

Help without ridicule, judgement, ego, high-mindedness or
expectation of repayment is help in its purest form.

-

"I was hungry and you gave me food, I was thirsty and you
gave me drink, a stranger and you welcomed me, naked and
you clothed me, ill and you cared for me, in prison and you
visited me."

Matthew 25: 34-40
****

Shariffe's dreads are gone!!! He is sporting a low bald fade
with a razor sharp outline and a freshly trimmed almost non-
existent beard. His head looks smaller and he has lost the
exotic strong natural look, which complimented his unique
personality, tall stature, muscular build and beautiful way of
thinking and living. Without his rich dark dreads he looks... he
plain, he looks just like every other ordinary man walking the
street. There is no more majesty and mystery surrounding him;
he no longer exudes the same exoticness that he once did.

"Why? Why did you cut your hair?"

"It was time," he says ambiguously. "Do you like it?"

"Yes," I lie. "It looks amazing, I love it. But just for the sake
of knowing, how long do you think it will take for you to grow
them back?"

He laughs, "I don't plan on growing them back but I know
how much you loved them so I kept the longest lock for you.
You can frame it or use it as a belt," he smirks.

His smile is still just as warm and captivating as ever, and
under the shadow of his long hair I never before noticed just
how long and curly his eyelashes are.

"No thank you," I laugh. "It's not the hair that impressed me, it was the man under the hair."

"I think that is the first nice thing you've said to me since we met," he smiles. "Annnd you bought me a gift!" He exclaims while focusing his gaze on my hands.

Jovial laughter surges from my mouth like light and warmth surging from the sun.

"Candice is going to love it," he continues with a smile.

"I really hope so," I say while holding up a shiny new pink Tiara and turning it from side to side so that he can see the full extent of its splendour.

"Trust me Vanessa, she will love it. The crown itself doesn't matter, she is going to love it because she loves and looks up to you. It's not always about the gift, often times it's about the giver. It's going to break her little heart when you leave," he sighs.

I laugh, "Ohh... So, I can leave now?"

"Of course, you could have left whenever you wanted to leave."

"But, but you," I inhale then exhale. "You said that you wouldn't let me leave."

"I know I did."

"So then?"

"So then what?"

"You imprisoned me. I mean, I'm okay with being imprisoned by you now but in the beginning I wanted to leave and you didn't let me, I was trapped."

"If you were trapped, I wasn't the one trapping you."

"Yes you were," I raise my voice in contempt. "Take responsibility Shariffe, I'm not mad at you but don't lie to yourself. You abducted and imprisoned me."

"In the beginning all I said to you Vanessa was that I am not allowing you to leave."

"Exactly, which means that you would do anything in your power to stop me from leaving."

"Wrong, Vanessa. It means that I would do any and everything within my character to stop you from leaving. I love having you here, I love spending time with you, I love your company and your spirit and I wanted and still want you to stay here with me, so of course I would do everything within my character to keep you here. I'm not perfect Vanessa but I try to maintain a character of love, so anything I would do to keep you here with me would centre around, and be fuelled by love, and love alone."

"You wouldn't understand because you're not a woman, Shariffe. Yes, you're a great man and yes I now know that you wouldn't harm a fly but in the beginning I didn't, and you never told me who you were. You made me figure out who you were over months. In the beginning if you had told me that I could walk out your mansion without being killed by you or eaten by your dogs I would have left the first day I got here but you didn't, you kept me in the dark."

"Vanessa, I told you over a dozen times that you weren't my prisoner. What else did you need me to say to prove that you weren't my prisoner? I left all the doors unlocked and I gave you innumerable opportunities to familiarize yourself with the dogs. I don't know what else I could have done," he laughs.

I open my mouth to wage war on his words when it hits me that what Shariffe did to me, the vagueness of his words and the ambiguity of his conduct, wasn't new or abnormal. What I experienced at the hands of Shariffe was the daily ambiguity and vagueness of life itself. Life never directly tells you what you can and cannot be, what you can and cannot do, where you can and cannot go, life simply creates opportunities and patterns and it is your duty to be aware of those opportunities and patterns and analyze them correctly. I think back to the first day I met Shariffe, I think back to everything that he did and said and I realize that I was misreading him and due to my misinterpretation of his personhood I missed out on what I wanted at the time.

I nod my head, "You're right, Shariffe. I created barriers for myself that weren't truly there. I was terrified of the outcome so I never went after what I desired."

"Sometimes you just have to close your eyes to your doubts and fears and just go for what you want."

"Well, I'm happy I didn't go for what I wanted in the beginning or I wouldn't be here right now and you'd probably be in the hospital or dead and at least one of your dogs would be dead."

"What?!" he looks at me in shock.

"Nothing, nothing," I laugh. "It was just a bad joke, I was never planning on hitting you over the head with a rock while we were gardening months ago and I was never ever planning on poisoning the dogs so that I could escape without being bitten."

We both laugh.

"So, have you decided what you're going to do once you leave here?" Shariffe says while staring intently into my eyes.

"I don't know, I haven't really thought about it to be honest."

"Well whatever you decide to do, I will pay for it," he half smiles. "Consider it a goodbye gift, no strings attached," he laughs a broken awkward laugh.

"I want to stay here," I blurt out without thought. "For Candice's sake," I continue quickly.

He smiles his rich, warm smile, "I was hoping you would say that. You can live here for as long as you would like... For Candice of course."

I laugh and step into his personal space. My body is tingling and I can feel the sexual tension between us rising. I glance at his chiselled arms and massive chest and can't help but imagine him scooping me up and blessing my lips with his lips.

"Vanessa," Shariffe says suddenly his eyes fiery and fierce.

"Yes, Shariffe," I say softly while batting my eyelashes and positioning myself in a position to be pounced on.

"Did you forgive Andrew? Did you help him? Please," he begs, his voice heavy with concern. "Tell me you helped him, Vanessa?"

"What?"

"Andrew!" he yells. "Vanessa, did you help Andrew?"

"Yes, yes, of course I did. I went over there and I told him how I felt and he did the same and then we hugged and forgave each other and now I feel free," I smile.

He exhales, releasing a heavy breath of air from his mouth, "Thank God... I... I guess I was wrong. I just received a really weird feeling in my spirit that something horrible is still going to happen."

"Nope, Andrew and I are in a good place, Shariffe. The crisis has been successfully averted," I laugh.

He hugs me and I lose myself in him. I want to squeeze his body, dig my fingers into his flesh like a shovel searching for gold.

"I'm really proud of you Vanessa. I don't know what he did to you but I can imagine how hard it must have been for you to forgive him."

"Ok, ok, new topic," I say, reluctantly freeing myself from the warmth of his embrace. "Where is my Candice and the other children? Shouldn't they be here by now?"

"The children aren't coming. Today you and I will be hosting an adults only celebration to acknowledge everything that God has done for us."

I roll my eyes, "Do you honestly believe that there exists some omnipotent, omniscient, and omnipresent being? Does that really make sense to you?"

"Yes," he nods his head.

I sigh and shake my head out of frustration. He and I could be the perfect couple if he would just free himself from this God delusion.

"If your God is all powerful and exists simultaneously in the past, the present, and the future then which version of your God is truly in control? Does your present God control the actions of your future and past God, or are all three of your Gods completely separate from each other, and if they are separate from each other then at what point in time does your past God become your present God and your present God become your future God?"

He laughs along with me but I am certain that he is not laughing for the same reason that I am laughing.

"Can God create a mountain so heavy that even He, Himself, cannot lift it?" Shariffe rambles. "Can God create a being who is more powerful than He is? Can God commit suicide? Does God grow old?"

I stare at him with a blank look on my face.

"There are certain questions, like the ones I just asked, which sound profound but these questions are in fact nonsensical. These questions seek to have God contradict His Own nature and character but if God altered His nature and character then He would no longer be God. So in essence these questions are asking if God were not God would God still be God? And the answer to that question is of course no; if God wasn't God then God would not be God but God is God and therefore He cannot and will not do ungodly things. God is not influenced by time, He is the creator of time... He influences time. When you think of God you have to try, albeit impossible, to think of Him outside of all of the phenomenon that influence you as a human."

I smile at his response, and although what he believes in is juvenile and absurd, the way in which he believes in what he believes is amazing and mature.

"Why are you like this?" I ask.

"Like what?"

"I don't know, you're just so," I struggle to think of the right words. "so... so different," I finally say. "Why are you so different?"

He chuckles, "The short answer to your question is Jesus Christ and I'll explain the long answer after the party. I don't want it to ruin your night."

"How will telling me what 'our God' did to make you the wonderful man that you are ruin my night?"

"I thought you didn't believe in God?"

"You convinced me," I smile.

"Me... I convinced you?" he raises his eyebrows in disbelief. "But, that's impossible, I can't-"

"Yes, yes, Shariffe," I interrupt, no longer desiring to debate him. "Everything you've said and done has convinced me. Now answer my question," I say sharply. "How will telling me what our wonderful God did for you ruin my night?"

He laughs, "Because the human brain is very powerful and yet very weak, it can rarely obtain new information without obsessing and coloring its world with that information. During the party, I want you to be in the moment, I want you to focus only on our guests and not on me."

Later in the evening, long after the house had been cleaned from top to bottom, and the solid white marble tables had been set with enough food to feed a small army, and long after the dark green grass had been neatly cut and watered, and long after Shariffe had finished praying, the front doorbell rings. Beaming with life I run to the large mahogany doors. Before opening the door, I look at myself in the mirror. I don't want to embarrass Shariffe or myself.

I take a deep breath.

I smile wide, displaying my polished white teeth, and then I pull the front door wide open.

All of the joy and excitement drains from my face.

"I'm sorry, but I think you must have the wrong address," I say quickly and then close back the front door and lock it before walking unhappily back to my seat.

"Who was it?"

"Some man, but he had the wrong address."

"What address was he looking for?"

"I don't know, I didn't ask."

"Then how do you know that this was the wrong address?"

Shariffe gets up, walks over to the front door and opens it.

I can hear him talking with the man and then seconds later he is standing in front of me with the man by his side.

"Make yourself comfortable sir. Vanessa and I will be sharing the food shortly. Would you like a drink while you wait?"

The filthy, urine scented, man shakes his head no. I'm relieved that he said no, I could only imagine the types of bacteria crawling and reproducing on his lips.

"Alright sir, well if you change your mind and would like a drink, the kitchen is right over there," Shariffe points. "Make yourself at home. I am going to pay the cab driver and see if maybe he will join us."

Shariffe walks off.

I look the man up and down in disgust then rise from my chair and storm after Shariffe.

"Shariffe," I say in an angry whisper. "What are you doing? Who is that?"

"I don't know him personally. I just handed him an invitation when I was downtown today."

"Are you crazy? Why would you invite him? The other guests are going to leave because of him."

He stares past me and looks at the man.

"What's wrong with him?"

"He stinks, I can smell him from here. His clothes are old and dirty, and he looks like he might be sick with something contagious," I snap quietly. "He has to leave, I don't want him ruining our party."

"So why don't you offer him a shower, give him some of my clothes and find out what medicine will cure his sickness? Instead of kicking him out why not invite him further in? Why judge him when you can help him?"

"But..." I sigh, digressing as I remember the shameful incident with Donovan a few days back. Although Shariffe never brings it up, I can feel it hanging over my head like a storm cloud, just waiting to burst. "Alright, alright."

I storm into the living room and stand in front of the dirty man. Shariffe and I will have to flip the sofa cushions over when he leaves and clean them with bleach and soap.

"You need to take a shower and change your clothes. You can't come to my party looking and smelling the way you do. You'll make the other guests uncomfortable. There is a washroom upstairs, let's go."

"Thank you," the man smiles revealing a row of crooked, yellowish white teeth and releasing a foul breath of air from his lips.

"I'll get you a toothbrush, toothpaste, mouthwash and some baking soda as well."

Unhappily, I lead the man upstairs. I imagine the horde of bacteria that must now be infecting the house because of him. What about the kids, what about Candice?! We will have to sterilize the whole house before we invite the children back over. As the man and I walk, he attempts to make small talk with me but I completely ignore him. When we arrive at the guest washroom there is a rag, a towel, an electric razor, a clump of African black soap, organic shampoo, a tooth brush, a green tube of pork free organic toothpaste, a small cup of baking powder and some clothes waiting on the washroom counter. I have no idea how or when he did it, but I guess Shariffe must have somehow gotten here before the man and I did.

"Please, keep everything that you use and wear. We don't want any of it back."

"Thank you so much, that is so kind and generous of you," he reaches out to shake my hand.

I look at his dirty fingers, his calloused palms and I want to hurl. I turn away and walk out of the washroom without touching the dirty man. When I enter the hallway, I hear the water from the shower begin to run. At least he still knows how to use a shower, I think to myself but the thought spirals into another thought and try as I might I can't stop myself from imagining the hordes of dirt, slime, and small insects that are falling from the man's unwashed body and threatening to clog the drain and stain the white porcelain tub.

We'll probably get cockroaches and rats and raccoons and pigeons and who knows what else.

I shake my head and grunt aloud.

Shariffe takes this good guy, love, and help the world thing too far. Does he have to help every person that he meets?

My heart begins to beat faster and my breaths become short and quick. I want to rip off all of the grotesque jewellery and the ugly fancy dress that I have on and just lock myself away in my room. I'm angry and sad but I don't know why. I don't know why it hurts me so much that Shariffe is willing to help a random homeless man. Maybe it is because deep down I know that I was once like the man, dirty and filthy and random, and that was probably how Shariffe saw me, and maybe still sees me.

I don't want to ruin Shariffe's special night so I fight the selfish urge to lock myself in my room. Putting Shariffe's happiness ahead of my own I head back downstairs, enter the living room, sit down, and allow my thoughts to consume me. Every nice thing that Shariffe has ever done for me becomes bitter sweet, pricking, and scratching abusively at my heart. I was nothing more than a project for some philanthropic rich man.

I'm not special.

I'm not his princess.

He doesn't love me.

Almost an hour later, my thoughts are disturbed by a loud sickly cough. When the man re-enters the living room, I am astonished by his transformation. His scruffy beard is gone. His ruddy hair is washed and maintained. He is wearing a gold watch, a nice pair of tan colored jeans, and a beautiful white cotton dress shirt that fits his skinny frame perfectly.

He sits down beside me and smiles.

His teeth are still yellow, and crooked, but at least his breath doesn't smell as horrible as it once did. I'm about to stand to my feet and search for Shariffe so that I can ask him what I should do next when I remember that I'm supposed to devote myself solely to the guests.

I sigh within myself and turn reluctantly to the homeless man and engage him.

His name is James Williamson. He used to be a successful, self-employed, carpenter until one day while riding his motorcycle, some six years ago, a car swerved into his lane, crashing into his bike and throwing his body into the air.

The driver sped off and was never caught.

James sustained major injuries to his back, his wrists and his hands. His injuries prevented him from working and completing the jobs that he had been hired to do, so he had to reimburse all of his customers who had paid him upfront. Three months after his accident, James swallowed his pride and he applied for assistance through the Ontario Disability Support Program but the government / taxpayer-funded program did not provide James with nearly enough money to cover his monthly bills or the cost of his medication. Eventually, he was cut off from his disability benefits because his doctor claimed that he was healthy enough to return to work despite the fact that James could barely hold a hammer. Before long, James was living on the streets and all because someone didn't care enough about other people to check their blind spots.

My eyes fill with tears, I'm able to relate to James' every word. His life is no different from my life. If when I was younger my mother had cared enough about me to check her blind spots, even just once, she would have seen that her desperate, and reckless actions were injuring me, and ruining my life. She would have understood that picking a man over me, ignoring me, and not showing me any love was slowly killing me. If she had checked her blind spots, she would have seen me begging, and crying out for change.

Just before tears pour over my eyelids, I take a deep breath and get a hold of myself and say, "Is there anything that I can do to help you James?"

"Could you lend me a million dollars?"

My mouth and eyes open wide in shock.

James erupts with a blast of laughter, "You've already helped me a lot. I just wish that more people in this world were like you and could understand that homeless doesn't equal worthless."

"I'm so sorry for the way I treated you earlier, James. You're an amazing person and I... I'm sorry," I hang and shake my head in shame.

"I forgive you Vanessa," James smiles at me, but this time his teeth are a glowing white, and the red lines that had once plagued his sclera are gone. His entire face emanates warm, bright light that seems to enter me. My entire body begins to tingle with life and tears start to pour from my eyes.

I close my eyes and shake my head in disbelief. When I reopen them, his eyes and teeth have gone back to their normal sickly state. I blink again and again, but nothing spectacular happens. His teeth, his eyes and the skin on his face remain dull and lifeless.

James stands to his feet, stretches his hand towards me, mouths something that I am unable to comprehend, and then walks off and blends in with the crowd of people who now fill the house.

A strange sensation rushes through my bones; it feels like an unstoppable yet peaceful fire that is threatening to consume all of me and as crazy as it sounds, I want to be consumed by this fire. As the feeling continues to rush throughout my body I can't take my eyes off of James. I can't help but watch him as he mingles with all of the other guests, making them laugh, and smile. I wonder, to myself, if the other guests would be so joyful to see James if he weren't clothed in the finest garments, smelling of high-end cologne, and sporting an expensive gold watch.

The night continues and although I have since lost sight of James in a sea of other guests, his words stick with me, and replay in my mind. I try to focus on the other guests, like Shariffe requested, but my brain won't allow me to greet or even look at a single guest without wondering about their blind spots. Wondering if he or she is living in somebody else's blind spot or if he or she has someone living in their blind spot. If he or she is here eating, drinking, talking, and laughing happily meanwhile some poor person is suffering because of their lack of care.

I need to speak with Shariffe. I search the entire house, from top to bottom for him, but he is nowhere to be found. I want to tell him all about James, and I want to ask him about the blind spots that exist in his life and tell him about the blind spot that I lived in all of my life.

CHAPTER 26

Saved

(Vanessa)

Take all the money, take all the gold, take all the diamonds
and material possessions on earth and they will not add up to
even one percent of your true worth.

-

*"For what shall it profit a man, if he shall gain the whole world,
and lose his own soul."*

Deuteronomy 32:39

****

As soon as the last guest has left Shariffe reappears like
magic. Grabbing hold of me, he hugs me tight, lifts me
effortlessly and spins me in the air before I can ask him about
his blind spots or tell him all about James.

"Preg. Baby, boy. Pregnant baby boy," Shariffe exclaims,
his face glowing as he spins me effortlessly.

"What are you talking about, Shariffe?" I laugh, when he
finally puts me down. "Take your time and try saying that
again."

With unabated joy painted across his face, he bellows out,
"She's pregnant! Vanessa, she's pregnant!"

"Who?" I ask in shock. "Who's pregnant?"

"Charles and Alice, the couple from the hospital whose son
passed away. They were at the party tonight and I prayed for
the both of them and God spoke to me, He told me that He will
bless them with a healthy baby boy," he smiles from ear to ear.

Without warning he takes me by the hand and leads me
upstairs. It is nearly two in the morning and after running
around all night tending to and speaking with dozens of guests
my feet are swollen, my back is aching, and I am worn out but
I ignore the pain and the fatigue and do my best to keep up
with a raptured Shariffe. When we arrive at my room, Shariffe
opens the door, turns on my light and tows me over to my bed

where the two of us sit. He slides the palm of his left hand over the back of my right hand causing my skin to come alive.

I inch closer to him, every centimeter of my body electrified by the anticipation of his embrace.

"I want to fulfill my promise to you, Vanessa. I want to tell you about my past, but I don't want my past to ruin our friendship or cause you to leave."

"I won't leave, I'll always be here with you. I don't care who you were or what you did in the past, all that matters to me is the great man that you are now."

He smiles his usual smile and then squeezes my hand tightly. In that single moment, as sensation, expectation, fulfillment and extreme jubilee shoot and explode like tiny rockets throughout my body, I realize that I am in love with Shariffe, and that the type of love I have for him is the type of love that has the ability to beautify monstrosities, and make inconsiderate tyrants seem tender-hearted. I have that nothing- in- this- world- can- make- me- stop- loving- you kind of love for Shariffe.

"I killed Candice's mom," he sighs.

My jaw drops wide open and time seems to stop as I sit paralyzed in the middle of my bed.

He releases my hand and looks to the ground, shaking his head, "It's a long story, Vanessa, but I feel you deserve to know it. I wanted to tell you from the beginning of our friendship but if I told you in the beginning that I killed someone you would have never come home with me, you would have written me off, you would have judged me. I just needed to show you-"

"Just tell me what happened, Shariffe," I cut in. "I don't care about why you didn't tell me."

He looks at the wooden bracelet that he is wearing around his wrist and for the first time since I met him, he seems to be completely vulnerable.

I hear the dogs bark and howl at something outside.

My left eye twitches.

He opens his mouth and I can't help but brace myself for impact.

"I wasn't born rich, Vanessa. My parents and I were extremely poor and I had to sacrifice a lot and hurt a lot of people to get everything that I now have. When I was younger I hated how my parents viewed life, their hearts were big but their minds were simple, they were okay working a 9 to 5 and coming home to a small apartment and barely making ends meet. They never questioned anything or attempted to break free from the devices of their oppression. They followed every rule, every law to the letter, it seemed as if they were just so happy to be in Canada, the land of opportunity, that they never thrived to get the fullness of what Canada had to offer. My parent's didn't want to take over the world and control their destinies and I always blamed this on their lack of education but more so on their religion. Books and research journals showed that the poor tend to be more religious than the rich, that the poor need to believe in God in order to cope with the stressors of life and keep from going insane. When poor people feel broken and powerless they like to create a powerful being that cannot be subjected to the abuses that they themselves are facing. When I was young I saw this quality in my parents. My parents were poor immigrants, my father was from Jamaica and my mother was from Cuba and they were both what you would call trans-generational Christians. They believed in Jesus Christ because their parents before them believed in God and raised them to believe in God. My parents didn't seek and find God, they inherited God the way a baby inherits the physical traits of his or her direct biological predecessors. Naturally, my parents expected me to continue the family tradition of holy blind belief and although this was problematic to me, I was young and I loved and believed in my parents so I tried to do things their way. I tried to believe without questioning but it was impossible for me to learn about something and develop a relationship with that thing if I didn't question the thoughts, actions, origin, and the motives of that thing. In order to love God I needed to know the character and mind of God. Serving a God I didn't know was no different than serving an idle. So I threw blind faith out the window and I started studying and asking questions.

Where did the bible come from?

Who was King James and why are we reading his version of the Bible?

How old is God?
Where did God come from?
Who gave birth to God?
Why does God get to be indiscriminately in charge?
Why don't angels get to vote and choose their God?
Why isn't heavan a democracy?
Does God get bored?

If God is always in a perfect state, If He has everything He wants then why did He one day want to create humans and planets and if God has wants and needs doesn't that make God imperfect or is it possible to want what you already have?

Did God create everything out of nothing or did He pull from His own essence in order to create all that currently exists?

When I asked these questions my parent's didn't have an answer. More than our poverty it troubled me that the people who were leading and directing my life were following rules, believing stories, and loving a God that they knew absolutely nothing about. So, at the age of seventeen I read the entire bible for myself. According to the bible, there is an All-Powerful Being who loves and protects humans who follow His commands. Every page of the bible seemed to promote God's love for His followers but I never saw this loving and generous God in reality. Instead, I saw a God who punished individuals for doing good and rewarded individuals for doing evil. In my neighbourhood drug dealers, gangsters, scammers, thieves, prostitutes and pimps drove around in expensive cars, wore fancy clothes and lived the high life meanwhile my mother and father struggled to survive," Shariffe sighs. "I eventually concluded that my parents were crazy and they needed me to free them from their God delusion, because who in their right mind would serve a God who allowed them to suffer?

One day I went to my mother with a history book and told her that there was no proof anywhere in history that HaMashiach Yeshua (Jesus Christ) existed. I told her that the bible was politically, socially and economically motivated. I showed her pages upon pages of historical data that proved that the bible didn't come from God or fall from heaven. I showed her proof that the Roman Emperor Constantine formed the bible as means to further enslave the minds of the proletariat. Constantine wanted to unify his kingdom and he used Christianity to do so, Christianity promoted subjection to rulers and the providence of God in the appointing of rulers. I showed her proof that Jesus didn't decide what books were going to be in the bible, Jesus didn't even write a single page of the bible. It was political and religious elites who manufactured what we today consider to be Holy Scripture. Then after the Romans the bible was translated and changed by King James and unknown groups of European writers. I told my mother that we might as well worship a tree because at least there was proof that the tree existed. At least the tree gave us shade, oxygen and possibly fruits, at least we could cut down the tree and build a house, at least the tree was useful."

'Who do you think gave you the tree?' My mother asked me.

"The earth," I answered her.

'And who gave you the Earth?'

"The stars, the universe, matter, energy. The Big Bang."

'And who gave you all of those things?' she asked me.

"I had no answer for that question but back then nothing would convince me that God existed unless God Himself physically appeared in front of me and proved himself by performing a list of ostentatious miracles. Back then I thought that not believing in God was the most liberating thing that a person could do. By not believing in God or eternal punishment I became master of my life, I stopped kneeling with my eyes closed and I started walking with my eyes open. I stopped praying to God for money and I got myself a job at a call center for a major Canadian bank. The bank didn't pay me nearly enough to satisfy all of my needs but despite being underpaid and overworked I continued working and doing the *right thing* until one day a client who owned multiple hotels and resorts in Montego Bay Jamaica phoned the call center. He had 17 million dollars sitting in his bank account, he had 17 million whole Canadian dollars just sitting there not doing anything with it meanwhile my parents and I had zero. Frustrated and tired of living paycheque to paycheque, while rich clients got more paycheques than they could spend, a couple of friends and I started stealing client information. We copied credit card numbers, online banking usernames and passwords. We emptied entire lines of credits and bank accounts," Shariffe shakes his head and sighs aloud. "After five years of working at the bank, I had seventy-eight thousand dollars sitting in my staff bank account, one-hundred-thousand dollars stashed in an iron safe in my room, two binders worth of credit card numbers, and other client information.

The end goal for me was always Law school, so when I had saved enough money I quit my job at the bank and I paid my way through university and then through Osgoode Law. I graduated and became a crown attorney. After winning my first case by lying to a jury of twelve, I remember thinking to myself that lying and stealing was necessary in order to survive in this modern world where illegal was the new legal and wrong was the new right. I did a lot of wrong and I told a lot of lies that destroyed a lot of lives and put a lot of innocent people in jail. Candice," his voice cracks.

I think I see a tear run from his eye, but I'm not certain. I move closer to him and take his hand in mine.

His hand is trembling.

I hold it tight.

I am here for him.

I don't care what he did.

I need him to know that nothing else matters but us. The bad decisions he made, the pain of his past, they all mean nothing to me.

'You hypocrite, how can you love a man who killed a woman?' My mind screams at me.

With bated breath, I ignore my mind and grip Shariffe's hand even tighter.

"Her mother is dead because of me," he says. "I killed her. She was convicted of drug possession with the intent of trafficking but I knew that she was innocent. The evidence pointed to Candice's father but he was nowhere to be found and he was some low level citizen that the government didn't care much about. The money and time that it would have taken to track him down wasn't worth it, it was easier to close the case and move on to a higher paying one, so I lied. I twisted and omitted evidence until everything pointed to Candice's mother," he shakes his head. "I rationalized it by saying that a woman who dates a man like that, a man with such low character, must be doing something illegal herself. There are consequences for associating with thugs and lowlife men and I wasn't going to waste my time keeping some woman out of jail that wasn't wise enough to make good life choices. My time was money and back then she wasn't worth a minute of it. In the courtroom I only thought about time and money it didn't matter to me if the defendant was guilty or not. Every good lawyer knows that there is no such thing as truth in a courtroom; judgements are based on the perception of truth not truth itself. Whenever I walked into a courtroom I could tell the judge and the jury whatever lies I wanted and they would believe me so long as I spoke eloquently, looked dignified, and told a good story that seemed to contain no holes and resonated with their culture, current situation in life or personal beliefs. I studied fashion, psychology and Eye-ology. I learned how to guess someone's income bracket based on the clothes they wore and the way in which they wore those clothes. I learned to see people's pain so that I could use their pain to control them. If I saw a juror who looked sickly or seemed to be suffering from depression I would relate depression and sickness to the case. If the jury was comprised of mainly women, I would workout every morning, spray on a specific cologne and I would whiten my teeth and smile as much as possible. It felt good knowing that I not only controlled my life but I also controlled the lives and perceptions of others. Everything was going perfect in my life. My family was financially stable and I had acquired the position that I felt I was born to inherit but sadly, while I was rising my Candice, my little precious princess, was falling. When Candice's mother went to jail, Candice was only three years old and had no other family to take care of her. I didn't know this at the time but even if I did, I wouldn't have cared. The only things I cared about back then were my parents, my money, my time and myself.

Overtime, I won many more cases, made a lot more money and I continued to succeed. I used a portion of my earnings to purchase acres of land and a small fleet of dump trucks. I used my money and power to acquire contracts for my dump trucks and then I hired drivers. I built houses on my land and then I turned my drivers and their families into my tenants so that I could have even more control over them. I was their boss and their landlord; I controlled where they lived and the money that they made. The only need that I didn't control was the food my employees ate, and I had plans to open up a grocery store so that I could control that also," he laughs. "Vanessa, back then my whole life was geared towards controlling people, I was in love with money but I only loved money because it brought me power. Power is so intoxicating, Vanessa. Until you have what seems to be supreme power of people, places, and things you will never understand how addictive and misleading it is. Even with you Vanessa, there were moments where it felt really good knowing that I had, what seemed to be control of your mind. I had to constantly remind myself that I'm not that man anymore. I don't want to control you or anyone but there is still apart of me that craves owning and controlling other people."

His words shock and disgust me, but they don't change how I feel about him. I still love him.

"I earned millions of dollars, I bought anything I wanted, went everywhere I wanted and got any woman I wanted but the best part was knowing that my parents no longer had to beg God for anything, all they had to do was call me and I would fulfill all of their needs," he shakes his head.

"Six months after Candice's mother was convicted, both my parents were murdered for a car that I had bought for them. They went back to our old neighbourhood in Jane and Finch to visit a friend and pray for their wayward son. While walking from their car to the building my parents were held up at gunpoint, robbed, and then shot.

My friend Robert, who you met at the police station, grew up with me on Jane and Finch and worked with me at the bank. At the time Robert still sold credit and client information to some of the young people in the area and he was able to find out who killed my parents.

When Robert caught the four kids who were responsible, he brought them to me. They could not have been older than seventeen, but I didn't care. I wanted revenge, I wanted them to suffer. Robert and I tied the kids up in my basement and for three weeks we beat them, tortured them, starved them, burned them and then we ensured that they were sentenced to life in prison without parole. I was filled with so much anger and hurt that I planned on having all of their parents killed, but Robert talked me out of it. He told me that their parents would suffer more knowing that their children would never be free again. So I let them live but once in awhile I would pay somebody a couple hundred dollars to add extra stress to their lives.

Nine months after burying my parents, when I was just beginning to heal from the wound of losing them, I woke up in the middle of the night in excruciating pain. When I arrived at the hospital they admitted me to the emergency room and two weeks later I was diagnosed with A.L.S."

Shariffe laughs as tears stream down his cheeks.

I want to ask him what A.L.S. is but I'm too afraid.

"What will it cost to fix me?" he continues speaking. "Those were my exact words. The doctor said to me that A.L.S. was not something that you fixed... it was something that you accepted. All my money and power was useless, I was going to die."

Everything slows down to a halt and a heavy feeling rushes to my stomach. The ground seems to shake beneath my feet and I start to sob and cry uncontrollably.

He squeezes my hand tenderly.

I turn away.

I don't want to hear anymore and I want to forget what I've already heard. I wish I had never asked him about his past.

"Stop," I say, pulling my hand from his grip. "Just stop."

"Don't worry Vanessa," he says, taking my hand back into his. "This isn't a sad story, it has a happy ending."

With tears in my eyes and the weight of the world crushing my weak heart, I turn and look him in his eyes.

"I became depressed and suicidal," he continues. "If I was going to die, I wanted to die on my terms. I wanted to die like a man. I didn't want my last days to be spent strapped to a hospital bed or hooked to plastic feeding tubes with some woman in blue scrubs bathing me with a sponge. I wanted my last days on earth to be enjoyable and an expression of my power and all that I had accomplished, so I searched the Internet for pleasurable ways to commit suicide and that's how I learned about the plant, aconitum. That night, after reading for hours about aconitum, and what to mix it with to ensure a quick and enjoyable death, I was lying in my bed trying to fall asleep when everything around me stopped. At first, I thought that it was the disease destroying my brain but then I heard a Voice. The Voice was rough but comforting and felt as if it was coming from without and within me at the same time.

The Voice asked me if this was proof enough for me and if I was finally ready to accomplish my true purpose. In tears I said yes, and then The Voice showed me the demon that had been whispering in my ears for the last twelve years, the demon that had been fuelling my pride, ego, anger and selfishness. I begged The Voice to remove the spirit and to heal me of my disease but The Voice said no. The demon and the disease would be with me until the day that I died. The Voice told me that I must reap what I have sewn, but that I should not worry or be afraid because He has also sewn for me, and the joy of His harvest is greater than the sorrow of my harvest."

I can't stop myself from crying, I want to ask him how he can be sure that his vision was real, how he can be sure that it wasn't the disease, his sorrow and lack of food that caused him to hallucinate?

"I fell asleep that night in awe of God's power," he continues. "Every single element and molecule had to bow, and show Him reverence. My money and my power was nothing compared to Him and His power.

The next morning, I woke up early and drove to the Ontario Court of Appeal to file motions to retry several of my cases. I was able to free some of the people who were innocent but by the time I got around to Candice's mother, it was too late, another inmate had killed her.

Ever since that day, I have done everything within my power to adopt Candice but because of my short life expectancy, all of my applications were rejected.

I felt discouraged but I refused to give up. I refused to let her suffer because of my mistakes, so I wrote a will, which ensures that upon the death of my flesh everything I own will be transferred to Candice and the person who God has chosen to take care of her.

I started the children's organization S.O.I.L. because I wanted to be as close to Candice as possible. I wanted her to become familiar with the house and the land that would one day be hers. Even the dogs are for her. She said she wanted dogs, really big dogs, so I went out and I bought her really big dogs but they're terrified of her and always run away whenever she tries to play with them," He laughs.

I try to laugh but I can't.

"She loves flowers," he says. "So I filled the entire house and yard with flowers. She means the world to me and I regret killing her mother but I don't regret helping and loving Candice. The part that troubles me is that I would have never cared, or loved in this way if I did not kill Candice's mother. Some people only become good, some people only want to help and love others," he says, tears running down his cheeks and soaking into his beautiful sky blue dress shirt. "After they have committed or experienced life-changing evils, I'm one of those people, Vanessa. We," he takes a deep breath then looks dead into my eyes, and squeezes my hand tightly. "We all go through situations that have the potential to either make us or break us, the choice is ours whether we will walk around broken or walk around made... I choose made."

He removes the wooden bracelet that he is wearing around his wrist and hands it to me.

"A.L.S." The three letters seem to cut my lips as they leave my mouth.

"Look closer," he smiles.

"All Loving Saviour."

"God's love and salvation is present in all things, even the things that we believe are killing us. We just have to look closer we just-"

"How the hell is he your *all loving saviour* when he isn't saving you!?" I snap.

"He has saved me."

"No he hasn't," I shoot back. "You're dying Shariffe."

"Only my flesh."

"You are your flesh," I yell. "When your flesh dies, you die!"

"No Vanessa," he says while shaking his head in a calm manner that makes me even more upset. "This body is only a shell. Everything that we see in this world is just a shell. There is a spirit, an invisible force, behind everything that exists in this physical world. You and I are both spirits who are going through a short humanistic experience. When the shell, that is my flesh, is no longer useful to my spirit then my spirit will discard it and move on. I am not concerned about the dying of my flesh, I am concerned about the living of my spirit."

I'm angry and frustrated. My head is throbbing and my heart is beating fast. This is too much for me. I open my mouth to respond but no words come out.

I start to cry.

I cry because I'm frustrated and I'm sad. I cry because he is dying and I have no power to stop death. I cry because I want him to know how wrong I think he is, I want him to know that nothing will ever convince me that some imaginary man in the sky loves him or me, but more than anything I cry because I want him to know that I'm in love with him and I refuse to live a single day without him, but try as I may the words refuse to come.

"Vanessa," he says softly. "I love you and I need you to understand that my love for you will never die, even when my flesh is dead and gone my love for you will still exist because my love for you does not come from or belong to my corruptible flesh. My love for you comes from an indestructible Source, which means I can and I will love you forever. I love you beyond your flesh and beyond my flesh, I love you with every ounce of my spirit."

Shariffe stands to his feet, reaches into his pant's pocket, and withdraws a beautiful yellow gold necklace. Dangling from the end of the necklace is a pair of diamond-encrusted wings. He clips the necklace around my neck, wipes the tears from my eyes and hugs me tightly before exiting my room.

Five months later, Shariffe was gone.

His passing from this life into whatever comes next was not quick or peaceful; there was no beauty, grace or dignity in his death. He did not utter philosophies and words of wisdom; he did not smile his corky smile before saying farewell poetically and then releasing a well timed exhale of final life. Instead, he coughed, groaned, cried out in pain, secreted odd coloured mucus and bled like a criminal who was being imprisoned and brutally beaten by his own body.

The disease began at Shariffe's legs, confining him to his bed then it moved upwards weakening every muscle in his body. Week by week the rich dark hue of his skin slowly dulled.
His sclera turned a sickly yellow, filled with red lines, and secreted a thick light green substance that I would have to wipe away or it would pile up, crust over, and hinder his sight. I was forced to watch life pour out of the man who had poured life into me.

Eventually, the disease finished destroying Shariffe's body and moved to his face, stiffening his tongue and destroying every muscle in his jaw and leaving the once talkative Shariffe, speechless.

I communicated with him through yes or no questions. He would blink once for yes and twice for no until one day he stopped blinking altogether.

When Shariffe's '*spirit*' broke '*free*' from his flesh, there was no epic struggle or fight to survive. Shariffe's body did not gyrate in rebellion; his hands did not shoot into the air as if hoping to grasp the tail end of some ungraspable thing; the sky did not open up and welcome him, his life just evaporated until all traces of it were gone.

This was the thing that I had sought, had desired, most of my adult life, this was death... the slow, inglorious, erasing of one's existence that one-day every human would have to face.

CHAPTER 27

DEATH

(Vanessa)

What is death but a thin gateway into an incomprehensible
infinity, the closing of one set of eyes and the opening of
another set of eyes, the removal of all veils and lies, the
penetration of darkness by light, the answering of that timeless
question that can only be answered once time itself is
removed?

-

Jesus said to her, "I am the resurrection and the life. Whoever
believes in me, though he die, yet shall he live, and everyone
who lives and believes in me shall never die."

John 11:24
****

Five days after Shariffe's passing his emaciated body was
placed into a simple wooden coffin and lowered into the earth.
Siting atop his flowerless grave was an inglorious tombstone.
Before his ability to speak had been completely stripped away
from him Shariffe made it clear to me that he did not want an
elaborate funeral that would glorify the spiritless body that he
would be leaving behind. Once his spirit left his body his body
was no different than the earth that it was being placed in and
he did not want a sturdy coffin that would prevent the earth
from reclaiming the material that it rightfully owned.
I argued with him for days attempting to convince him that he
deserved flowers, crowds of mourners, music and all of the
amenities, he deserved more than a thin plain box. I pleaded
and I begged, I told him that everybody whom he had helped
should be at his funeral but Shariffe refused. Eventually, I
submitted to Shariffe's demands meanwhile secretly planning
to go against his dying wishes when it was too late for him to
object but when the time finally came I just couldn't bring
myself to go against the dying desires of the man I loved. So

just as Shariffe requested, at his funeral, only I was there.

***

Only three days have passed since Shariffe's funeral and already I feel myself unhinging. Loneliness has never felt more real than it does right now at this very moment. I want... I need Shariffe to come back to me. I need the earth to open up and give him back to me. I see myself using my bare hands to dig up his grave and then by some miracle willing him back to life with my love.

I wish fairy tales were real.

I wish Shariffe's man in the sky existed and would hear my cries and resurrect him.

Tears stream down my cheeks.

A voice in my head tells me that I don't deserve to cry, that Shariffe's death is my fault and although I know deep in my heart that I'm not to be blamed I still can't help feeling guilty. The voice shows me images of a fat and lazy me lying in bed while Shariffe runs around cooking and cleaning. The voice tells me that I placed added stress on his already weak body. It shows me glimpses of his trembling arms and the constant times he tripped and fell over his own feet. It tells me that if I weren't so selfish and stupid I would have noticed that he was sick. It tells me that Shariffe should still be alive and I should be dead.

I agree with the voice, the hurtful words that it screams at me are all true.

An hour passes.

I'm tired of staring at the blackness that sits in my room so I rise from my bed and walk to my window. I pull the long white curtain to one side.

It is raining outside.

Shariffe's body must be soaking wet. His casket wouldn't hold up against this kind of a downpour. The wood was cheap and thin just like he requested.

How can you be gone?

How can you be dead?

How can so much life and so much love just evaporate into thin air?

-'Vanessa, I'm not dead.' -

I turn quickly.
Shariffe is standing at my room door holding a shovel and some seeds in his hand. Every cell in my body wants to run to him and hold him, but I control myself. He smiles his usual smile, sprinkles the seeds on my floor and then fades away. The seeds never grow.
He has been coming to me every day at the same time since his death. I try to stop him from coming only because it hurts too much when he leaves again. I stagger back to bed, curl up in a ball, and listen to the gentle tapping of the rainfall against my window.
I close my eyes.

*

When I reopen my eyes I'm standing in a massive, beautiful, garden. Red and blue birds are flying all around me. The sun is shining, the sky is crystal blue and he is holding me the way I have always wanted him to hold me. Squeezing him tightly and filling my nose with his scent, I speak the three words that I thought I would never get the chance to say.
"I love you."
Shariffe releases me from his grip and backs away.
"Why do you love me?" he asks.
Teary eyed I begin to list off all of his amazing qualities along with every thoughtful and loving thing that he has ever done for me. As I speak, his skin loses its hue and starts to wrinkle, time passes quickly on his face and stress enters his eyes turning them a sickly yellow. I stop speaking and grab for his arm but it dissolves in my hand.
"What… What's happening?" I cry out.
"Keep going," he smiles weakly. "Keep going. What else do you love about me?"
"No," I shake my head.
"Trust me," he says.
"Promise me you won't leave me again."
"Promise me you'll see me."

"I promise, I promise," I cry. "Just please, please promise me that you won't leave again."

"I promise," he smiles but it's not his usual smile. His gums are black, some of his teeth are missing and the teeth that remain in his mouth are thin and yellow.

I can't stand to look at him, I can't stand to see him like this so I close my eyes and turn my head away from him but I can still smell his rotting flesh and decaying teeth.

"Vanessa, please," his voice is tired and feeble. "Why do you love me?"

"Because you loved me first," I almost scream. "Because you actually, genuinely loved me. Even when I didn't love myself, when I hated myself, you loved me. When I was rude and horrible to you... you," my voice cracks. "You loved me when I believed I was unlovable."

He smiles, opens his mouth to speak but no words come out, instead his beautiful lips crumble, a long line shoots up his chiselled jaw causing it to fall from the rest of his face. Every part of him collapses and dissolves until nothing more than a small pile of dirt is left in his place.

"Do you still love me, Vanessa?" A strange voice echoes from the pile of dirt, and everything in the garden stops moving and goes silent.

I try to respond but there are no thoughts in my head or words in my mouth. Suddenly, the pile of dirt begins to travail, it groans and it cries like a man who is suffering excruciating pain. A leg forms from the dirt and then an arm materializes. One by one, body parts emerge from the dirt mound until standing in front of me is my Shariffe.

"Vanessa," his voice is back to normal and the Garden is once again filled with noise and activity. "You don't love me Vanessa, you never have."

"Yes I do! I do love you!"

"No, you don't Vanessa." He says rough and emotionless. "You don't even know me. What you've grown to know and love is an image of me, a feeble representation of who I really am. You are in love with this body, this voice and these clothes. You're in love with my shadow, not me. I did everything I could to show you who I am but you refused to see me for me. You only saw what you wanted to see

Vanessa. Who am I to you Vanessa?"
I stare at him tongue-tied and enraged. How can he be so cruel? How can he look me in my tear filled eyes and say all of these horrible things to me? Especially after I spent the last five months of my life helping to take care of him, cleaning up after him, bathing him whenever he made a mess of himself. I didn't even complain when I had to change his diapers, his sheets and his clothes. My entire body is shaking with unimaginable anger. I want to scream and shout at him, I want to beat on his chest with my clenched fists until he admits that I was good to him, that I cared about him more than I cared about myself, that I loved him to the best of my ability.

"The greatest thing in life is to love and be loved in return, Vanessa. And when you love someone you have to be willing to allow that person to look inside of you and you also have to be willing to look inside of that person when they open themselves up to you, and no matter what you see you have to place your love in there, in that person, among all of the horror and the good that you see. I opened myself up to you but you never truly looked inside." A tear runs from Shariffe's eye, "I love you Vanessa and I'll never stop loving you."

I reach out to embrace him, but it is too late. His body dissolves in front of my eyes, leaving nothing in its place but a pile of dirt.

*

I wake up crying and screaming Shariffe's name. I try desperately to hold onto the dream, to the sensation of his touch but in a matter of moments it all escapes me. Shariffe is gone and my body is now void of the lingering of his embrace. All of the pain comes flooding back to me leaving me sadder and lonelier than ever. I close my eyes and keep them closed until the silence of my room is replaced once again with Shariffe's soothing voice... I run into his arms.

Hours later, I open my eyes. The black sky is gone and sunlight shines bitterly into my room. I'm about to force myself back to sleep when the sound of a bird chirping captures my attention. Remembering the two love struck cardinals, I rise from my bed and peer out my window. The small female cardinal is perched peacefully on my stone ledge. I look around for her male lover but he is nowhere to be found. Suddenly, memories of disgust, Donovan, blood, a mess of red feathers, and a little bird's mangled body fill my mind.

"How... How do you do it? How can you still fly after what you've been through?" I mumble, my face pressed hard against my window. "How, do you keep going after losing the one you love?"

Why had Shariffe done this to me? Why did he place these feelings and these desires inside of me, why did he show me a new part of myself only to cast that part of me back into darkness, why did he make me fall in love with him if he knew he was going to die? Why didn't he leave me alone like I had begged him to do in the beginning? If he loved me, he would have never done this to me. If he loved me, he would have told me from the beginning that he was dying. If he loved me he would have given me a choice but instead he forced me to live with him and only told me that he was dying when he knew that I was too emotionally invested to walkaway. He manipulated and played with me like I were a fool.

"I hate you, Shariffe! I hate you!" I scream, throwing my fists against my window.

The little bird flies off in fright.

I sigh and groan in pain. I can feel the pain in my chest leaking out of me and burning my skin.

'Jump,' the voice in my head returns.

'Jump...'

'Die...'

I open my room window.

I inhale and exhale deeply.

This is it.

This is the end.

I bite my bottom lip and lean forward. I'm about to release my grip on my walls and allow my body to fall when I see the small, female cardinal fly into a large tree and perch onto a thick bough next to a straw nest. Inside of the nest are three newly hatched baby birds. I watch her as she feeds her featherless chicks a large worm, before flying back into the garden and searching for more food. My whole body collapses and I fall to my room floor, weeping out loud while struggling to catch my breath. I'm the one who is heartless and selfish. All I ever do is complain. All I ever do is think about my own pain and all the horrible things that other people have done to me. I only focus on what I don't have and what I think I deserve to have. I never appreciate what I do have. I have never put my hurt and my pain aside for the sake of helping and loving others. I was so self-absorbed and blinded by my pain that I couldn't see all the things in my life that still deserved and required my love, I couldn't see the nest of young, beautiful lives that I was now responsible for. Shariffe was right, I never loved him, I only loved an image of him. I loved the fact that he treated me like a princess, I loved the fact that he cooked and cleaned for me and made me smile and laugh but I only loved him for what he was doing for me and not for what he was doing outside of interactions, I loved him selfishly. I loved the shell of the man and not what the man truly stood for. If I truly loved Shariffe I wouldn't stop living just because he was dead, I would continue living and I would take care of and add to everything that he had built when he was alive. If I truly loved Shariffe I would tend to his children, I would love Candice the way that he loved her and I would be willing to live and die for her if necessary. If I truly loved Shariffe then I would live for him by living the type of life that he had lived when he was alive.

CHAPTER 28

TRUTH
(Vanessa)

What is truth? Where does it come from? Whose truth is truest? What makes somebody's reality the accepted norm and another's reality something to be despised, ridiculed, and scorned?

-

Then said Jesus to those Jews which believed on him, "If ye continue in my word, then are ye my disciples indeed; And ye shall know the truth, and the truth shall make you free."

John 8:31-32
****

While the children run excitedly from floor to floor, and room-to-room, I stand in the kitchen, chopping up a wide assortment of fruits and vegetables for lunch. I now understand why Shariffe found so much joy in being around children. It is a child's carefree nature, the tenacity yet elasticity of a child's spirit. It is child's ability to live every day as if the problems and heartaches of yesterday have been washed away by the bright rays of a new day. It is a child's ability to forgive, forget, and move on without looking back.

"Where is he? Where is he? I searched everywhere, I looked in every room but I can't find him. Where is he hiding?"

My heart breaks a million times over. Without looking, I know exactly whom the words belong to. I put down the knife, turn around, and bend down so that I'm at eye level with her. I recite the words in my head before I say them aloud, trying to find the best way to say what I know needs to be said.

"Candice honey…Shariffe isn't…" Tears begin to fall from my eyes. There is no right way to present death. No matter how much you beautify and sugar coat death, it remains ugly and bitter and foul. "Shariffe isn't here anymore."

"Why did he leave? Where did he go? When is he coming back?"

I'm crying and sobbing uncontrollably as Candice stares at me in confusion, waiting for a time, a date, and a location that I know I can't give.

"What's wrong?" She asks.

Everything is wrong Candice. You're too young to understand but this is not how life is supposed to be. I shouldn't have to speak to you about death when you've just barely started to live. I shouldn't have to tell you that the person who you love is gone and that you'll never see him again no matter how much you cry or hope or pray. Worst of all, if the adoption papers go through successfully, how could I reveal to you that Shariffe was the reason why you needed to be adopted in the first place? No, this isn't how life is supposed to be but sadly this is the way that life is and I can't do anything to change the truth... unless... unless I lie. What if there was a God, what if when Candice died she would get wings and get to see Shariffe again, what if I could keep her heart from being broken? What if Shariffe was a great man who never did a single thing wrong, and what if he decided to sacrifice his perfect life for Candice only because he loved her more than he loved himself? What if he decided to open the children's camp because some gigantic jolly man in the sky had told him to do it and not because he felt responsible for the death of Candice's mother?

Truth is relative and whatever I tell Candice will be her truth and she will use that truth to build her reality and herself. Suddenly, in that moment, I began to understand and respect religion. Religion wasn't only created to control and manipulate, it was also created to soothe and make a purposeless life liveable. It was made for children and for those adults who were too afraid to face the perils of life without having an all powerful, all loving protector guiding their every step.

I sigh gravely, and compose myself. I want desperately to do it but I can't. I can't lie to her. She deserves to know the truth.

"Shariffe isn't coming back Candice, because he is dead. He's gone forever."

"He's gone to be with God in heaven forever?" Candice
beams with life, twisting my words in order to make them fit
neatly into her world and her reality.

I sigh again and speak as softly and compassionately as I
can, "No sweetheart, God isn't real and neither is heaven."
Her face contorts with anger and shock. Tears pool in her
eyes and I can feel my heart further breaking as I watch her
world begin to crumble.

"Yes they are! They are real!" She screams. "Shariffe said
that they are real and, and, and..."

I don't know what to do or say next so I open my arms and
reach for her, hoping that a hug will calm her down and show
her that even if God isn't real, I am real and I love her. I will
take care of her; I will hug her, and tend to her for the rest of
her life if she needs me to. She doesn't need God or heaven,
she and I can make this place our heaven and we can be our
own gods. I want to tell her all of these things while hugging
her but she steps back angrily, resisting my embrace.

"I don't believe you," she pouts. "You're a liar! You're a big
fat liar. God is real, heaven is real and, and, and Shariffe isn't
dead he is in heaven with Jesus. You, you, you," she stutters.
"You said I wasn't real and you... you said that I wasn't a
princess but I am. You and Shariffe both said I am,
remember?" From her head, she takes off the little plastic
crown that I purchased for her at a local toyshop and hands it
to me.

Staring deep into Candice's tear filled eyes I can see and
feel something that I have never seen or felt before. Past all of
her rage and her sadness is something real and pure,
something that has yet to be broken and ravished by this cruel
and deceitful world.

"Don't... Don't you remember?" Candice sobs. "I am a
princess, I am real... aren't I?"

"Of course you are! And of course I remember! How could I
ever forget?" I exclaim with a large, jovial, smile. "I was testing
you Princess because a lot of people are going to tell you that
you're not a princess and that there is no heaven and no God,
but you have to be strong ok? You have to keep on believing
in what you believe in even if the entire world tells you that
you're wrong, even if I tell you that you're wrong," I sniffle,

struggling to hold back tears. "You have to keep believing. You have to keep loving yourself and loving what makes you happy."

She nods her head, smiles a big smile and then hugs me. This hug is more important to me than any truth. Some lies are necessary. A lie that heals and builds must be better than a truth that wounds and destroys. For this one single hug I would tell a million lies, I would cover up a million horrors and I would beautify a million monsters.

"Now, how about you and I go sit and talk Princess Candice?" I hand her back her crown and she receives it with delight, placing it snug on her head. "I want you to tell me everything that you know about God and heaven and then I want you to tell me all of the amazing and fun things that you think Shariffe is doing in heaven right now with God. Do you think he is flying around, do you think Shariffe has wings?"

EPILOGUE

REVELATION
(Vanessa)

Do not deny the abundant evidence of God that rhythmically
beats within you and beautifully blossoms all around you.

"For since the creation of the world God's invisible qualities—
his eternal power and divine nature—have been clearly seen,
being understood from what has been made, so that people
are without excuse."

Romans 1:20
****

- Two Months Later -

I tip toe into Candice's room, stand inches from her bed, and
watch her while she sleeps. Every morning before going
outside and working in the garden, I sneak a peak at her. I
realize now that Candice is that special part of me that was
stolen from me by Andrew but given back to me by Shariffe.
Suddenly a strange sensation rushes through my body and
tears begin to roll from my eyes and I cannot hold back my
sobs this morning.
    Candice stirs awake, "Why are you crying?"
    "Because I'm happy, Princess."
    "You cry when you're happy?" Candice asks, her face
contorting in confusion.
    "Only sometimes. Only when I'm really happy." I raise my
hands to my face and wipe away my tears. "Would you like to
come outside with me and help in the garden?"
    "Ewww, Princesses don't play in dirt," Candice says sternly.
    "Buuuut I'll make an exce... exce... exception for you if you
make me blueberry pancakes," Candice smiles.

I laugh aloud, "Okay your majesty I'll make you pancakes and maybe I'll even make you a Mud Castle for you to live in and a mud bed for you to sleep on."

"Yuck," Candice giggles.

***

When Candice and I arrive outside the sun welcomes the both of us, wrapping us in its warmth. Before I can divide the workload and tell Candice what I need her help with, Candice scurries off, chasing after the three dogs.

I laugh to myself and smile as I watch her, she is happy and carefree and I want to do everything in my power to keep her that way.

I enter the garden alone, carrying a bag of seeds on my shoulder and a shovel and a hoe in my left hand. I dive right in, digging holes, pulling weeds, collecting worms and planting seeds. There is something therapeutic and transcendent about gardening, the act of opening up the earth and placing in it a living item that if tended correctly will eventually blossom and grow into a thing that can reciprocate the tenderness placed into it.

My cell phone rings and buzzes in my pant's pocket. I stick my silver hoe into the soft earth before wiping my muddy hands on the front of my shirt and reaching into my right pocket to retrieve my phone.

It's Andrew.

Rage and hatred invade me, eating away at my tranquility. I'm about to answer the phone and scream at Andrew. I want to tell him how much he hurt me and how much I in return hate him but I control myself, I realize that he will continue to overpower me if I give him the power to do so.

I tap the red ignore button, from this moment onward Andrew is dead to me. He will no longer have a hold on my life and, I refuse to allow him to rob me of my adulthood the way he robbed me of my childhood.

I exhale, place my hand on my heart and say, "Andrew, you are not allowed in here. I will no longer allow my hate to open my heart to your destruction."

I go to slide my phone back in my pocket but it slips clumsily from my hand, falls onto a large grey rock, and breaks apart. Picking up the dismembered pieces of my phone, I clean off clumps of wet dirt before placing the battery pack back inside of my phone and carefully clicking all of the pieces back together.

I press and hold down the power button.

The phone lights up with life, makes a loud whistling sound, and then turns back on as if nothing had happened.

Seeing my phone once again flowing with life my mind begins to run wild. I begin think about Shariffe's body atrophying in front of my eyes, his life being sucked out of him until he was nothing more than a withered mass of flesh. I think about Gwen Lucken and all of the other dismembered victims of serial killers like Leonard Diopold. I think about the poor cardinal whose tattered, dead, body I had accidently stepped on while rushing to get rid of Donovan.

When living creatures were taken apart nothing could put them back together, when they were turned off nothing could turn them back on. When they fell apart something special, a spark of life, an intangible energy, a spirit, a soul, an animating force left them and went somewhere else. No doctor or scientist could grab hold of that life force and place it back into a dead body the way that I could place a battery back into a phone.

I look around my garden, intrigued by the vessels of life scurrying and growing all around me. What does the animating force that gives humans life look like? Is it bigger and smaller in some people or is it the same size in every person? What if what Shariffe had said about conscious, invisible, spirits influencing human actions and thoughts was true? What if there was an invisible world beyond this visible world? What if there is more to life than what I can see? What if my body is the phone and there is an infinite battery, an unlimited power source inside of me?

Whose hand is my battery in?

I laugh away the crazy thoughts and remind myself that I am an adult woman, with real responsibilities, and I have no time to think about or succumb to fairy tales.

One hour later, my work in the garden is finally complete. I stand to my feet and look around in awe. A gentle, slow moving draught blows through the organic wall of green and brown that surrounds me. The calm movement of air brushes against my skin, cooling it momentarily.

'You cannot see the wind but the wind is always here,' a strange thought materializes in my head. 'It is always moving around you and it will always be exist even if you cannot perceive it. The wind's existence does not decrease or increase do to your ability or inability to see it, feel it, smell it, hear it or taste it at a particular instance in time. The wind's existence does not respond to your willingness to acknowledge it.'

I wrestle with the thought but before I can subdue and dispel it another thought enters and takes hold of my mind.

'How horrible could God be if the person who loved me the most and who I loved the most claimed that all of his love came from God, and what if experiencing the God that Shariffe worshipped was supposed to be done with something beyond my humanistic five senses? There are millions of people in this world who are unable to hear, touch, see, smell or taste; maybe there is a neglected sixth sense that allows mankind, regardless of physical ailment, intellectual prowess or economic status, to experience God.'

The thoughts are flooding my head now, stampeding through my mind like an unstoppable herd of wild elephants. Desperately, I try to put up a wall to keep them out but the thoughts break through effortlessly.

'My daughter, look around you,' I hear a Voice say. 'Observe your garden; look at the good work which you have just planted. The garden grows and it looks a specific way because of your handiwork. Each flower is positioned in an exact location not by accident or a series of abnormal inconsequential coincidences, but by your hands for your purpose. Just like My hands have positioned everything on this planet and in this universe for My purpose, and My purpose is love and truth and therefor your purpose is love and truth.'

Instantly, everything in my world begins to unravel and I find myself in a place, in a moment of peace that exceeds my understanding and my ability to explain. In that unexplainable foreign place my eyes are finally opened and the veil that has kept me from truly seeing and truly connecting with God is finally removed.

I now understand.

The things of the earth, which had no freewill, were stuck in a perpetual cycle of provisional love. Trees gave oxygen, shade and fruit, the sun gave light and warmth, the soil gave crops, the crops died and became a part of the soil, and the cycle continued over and over again. These things never disputed their purpose nor desired to hold back a portion of itself due to anger, bitterness or ignorance. Trees don't stop producing fruits or oxygen because their mad at you. Humans on the other hand are creatures who willingly take and then seek methods in which they can avoid giving back and this is because humans have the beautiful, yet dangerously ugly ability to choose.

'Only through God's absolute love could a devil be born, empowered and sustained,' I now understand exactly what Shariffe meant by that saying.

If God were a controlling, cruel, tyrant He would have never allowed Lucifer, the devil, one of His most beloved and powerful angels to have the freedom to choose his own path.

Freewill was the ultimate problem and the ultimate solution. Freewill gave every human the ability to do the opposite of God's will, which is the opposite of love and truth. And because humans can't physically see God but they can physically see other humans most humans often base their belief in God, not off of what God does, but off of what other humans do. Many people conclude that there is no God simply because some of the people who claim to be physical manifestations of God's purpose, are the furthest things from God's manifested will.

"I get it, I get it," I cry.

God's will is not rape; it cannot and could never be rape. By the very design of God's character, He will never force Himself or His will onto anyone.

I look around, analyzing everything from the dirt beneath my feet, to the plants, and the unseen roots that filled their visible green foliage with life. If I want to see what sustains the plants I have to dig deeper, just like if I want to see my own roots and the true source of my life, I will have to dig deeper than this surface, physical, world.

I inhale (taking).

I exhale (giving)

I take off my shoes and dig my naked toes deep into the rich dark soil of the earth. As the soft, wet, dirt mushes between my toes I realize that God has been showing me, on a daily basis, signs of His existence but because of my pain and my hurt I ignored God's proof. But God, refusing to relent in His pursuit of me, placed His loving proof and infinite truth into a man who I could not ignore. An ordinary man, who empowered by God's Holy Spirit became extraordinary and showed me the positive purpose of my pain, and made my past problems seem insignificant by positioning me in the light of my future glories but sadly I fell in love with the man when I was supposed to fall in love with the God who was influencing and operating within the man.

I drop to my knees, throw my hands in the air and begin to cry out in unabated worship of my Creator.

God is all around me.

God's proof is everywhere.

All of creation is proof of God, the intricate relationship between organisms is proof of God, life is proof of God, my thoughts are proof of God, the love Shariffe had for me was proof of God, I am proof of God.

Suddenly, the vibrating of my cellphone drags me from my thoughts. By the time I am composed enough to pull the phone out of my pant's pocket, the caller has already hung up and left a voice message.

I check the message.

It's Andrew.

He is crying and blubbering incoherently.

I turn up the volume on my phone and listen closely.

My stomach knots, and my heart cracks and breaks in two as I listen to his words. He is confessing to molesting another child, a little girl who delivers newspapers to his house. I... I remember the young child... I remember something within me telling me to warn the child, and I remember ignoring that thing. I remember Shariffe telling me that something horrible was going to happen... but I thought he meant to Andrew... I thought...

Tears roll down my cheeks.

My legs feel as if they are about to give out.

'This is your fault,' a voice says. 'You could have prevented this, you could have saved her but you chose not to.'

My eyes fill with more tears. The heavy burden of guilt rains down on me as I think about the poor little girl. Rape is something that no child, no human, no animal, no being should have to experience. Rape is grisly, rape is the worst form of intrusion; it is the most brazen form of robbery that a vile criminal can perform.

The horrid voice message ends with Andrew stating, amidst tears, that he enjoyed doing it, that he loved every single second of it, and that he doesn't think he can, or wants to stop. He says that he is a monster and that he does not deserve to live. He tells me that he is sorry for all that he put me through as a child, and then he promises me that I will never hear from him again because he has finally decided to do what he should have done years ago... kill himself.

A small quiet thought rises in my head, 'Save him...'

Another thought rises in my head, a louder, more appealing, more satisfying thought, 'Let him die, let him kill himself, he doesn't deserve to be alive...'

To be continued:

Book number 2:
A Misguided Heart

Thank you for purchasing and reading this novel to the end. I
appreciate your support. Please tell a friend about this novel if you
enjoyed it and please feel free to contact me with any enquires,
my details are below.

Damion Platt

Damion.Platt@gmail.com
Facebook: Damion Platt
Twitter: Damion Platt
Instagram: Damion Platt

Made in the USA
Columbia, SC
14 June 2017